Not The Girl They Expected

Verses Kindler Publication

Verses Kindler Publication.

Website: www.verseskindlerpublication.com

Not The Girl They Expected
By: Priya Bhuyan

ISBN: 978-93-47494-25-3

1st Edition

Price: INR 249/$13

Disclaimer

Not The Girl They Expected is authored by Priya Bhuyan. The entirety of this published work comprises the original content of the author, who has undertaken diligent efforts in its editing. The characters depicted herein may be fictitious or inspired by real events; however, they are not intended to cause offense or represent any prejudice against any caste or system. Any similarity to the names of actual individuals, locations, or institutions is purely coincidental and serves the narrative. The author bears sole responsibility for the originality of this work; the publisher assumes no liability thereof.

Index

DEDICATION

To every woman who was told she was too much,

too loud, too ambitious, too emotional,

and kept going anyway.

To the girl who grew up being asked, "Why weren't you a boy?" and learned to make space for herself when no one else would.

To the mothers who carried more than their share,

to the sisters who stood like walls when the world shook,

and to the daughters who watched, learned, and rose.

This is not a story of perfection.

This is a story of persistence; quiet, fierce, and unshakable.

Of women who didn't ask for permission, but made their own way.

If you've ever been made to feel less,

I hope these pages remind you:

You were never less to begin with.

PREFACE

There were many times I was told to adjust, to endure, to not speak too much, feel too deeply, or aim too high. I listened for a while. Then slowly, I began to question.

This book is not about proving anyone wrong. It is about becoming who I was meant to be; without apology, without fear, and without waiting for the world to agree.

I was not born into ideal conditions. I did not grow up with a clear path. But I was born with something I couldn't name back then, a quiet force that refused to give up. It showed up as persistence in school, as stillness in struggle, and later, as service in my work.

Writing these pages was not easy. Revisiting some memories felt like walking barefoot over old glass. But I wrote them because I know I am not the only one. There are so many others, carrying their own battles, wondering if they have the right to dream beyond survival. This is my story. But if you find even a small reflection of yourself in these chapters, then it has done what it was meant to do.

-Lakshmipriya

PART I - ROOTS AND RISE

Chapter 1: Born Unwelcome, Raised Unbroken

"I am not what happened to me, I am what I choose to become."

Carl Jung, Swiss psychoanalyst

They say some births change the course of a family. Mine arrived wrapped in contradiction.

The day I was born, a letter arrived for my father, his first government job. In a village where such jobs were golden tickets out of poverty, this news lit up the room. As for me, a firstborn daughter, the response was polite and subdued; neither disappointment nor celebration was evident. "At least she's healthy," someone said. "Maybe the next will be a boy." My father held me gently, his attention already drifting to the envelope in his hand. Some called it divine timing; a girl born just as fortune knocked on the door. But it was the job, not my arrival, that brought the real joy.

But luck is a strange thing. To my father, I was auspicious. To the rest of the family, I was a disappointment. The son they had longed for, prayed for, pressured my mother for; never came. Instead, I did.

No songs were sung for my birth. No sweets were distributed. My arrival was met with silence, like a guest no one wanted to receive. That silence would stay with me. It clung to the walls of my childhood like dust no one bothered to sweep away.

Even as a child, I could sense it; I wasn't exactly what they had hoped for. Had I been a boy, it might have been different. There were no celebrations, just quiet acceptance. But within that silence, something else began to grow. It wasn't shame or fear, but something steadier, a small voice that didn't come from around me, but from within. I couldn't name it then, but I felt it: You are here for a reason.

Even before I knew the word for it, I understood denial. It lived in the way people's eyes plunged past mine, in the stillnesses that assembled behind me like clouds, in discussions that terminated the moment I stepped into a room. I didn't have the terminology yet, but I knew what it meant to be imperceptible.

I remember one afternoon vividly. I was sitting at the edge of the courtyard, knees scraped and dust coating my legs. My grandmother was laughing as she fed a portion of jaggery to the neighbour's son. She dabbed a bit on his cheek and said, "May your sweetness bring luck to this house." I smiled, quietly optimistic, and walked toward her. I didn't ask for anything. I just stood there, waiting to be noticed. She didn't even glance at me. "Go inside," she said snappily. "Girls shouldn't loiter like this."

I turned and walked back slowly, head low, the sweetness I never received projecting like a lump in my throat. That day, I learned what bitterness tastes like when you're too young to name it.

There was always a reason to remind us of our place. We were too loud, too wild, too much. My mother had long stopped trying to please herself; she was too busy trying to please everyone else. Still, they told her to try again, for a son. She did. Twice. First came I, then my younger sister. To her, we were a blessing. To the world, we were failures stacked one after another.

I remember her third pregnancy clearly. The air in the house turned dense. Relatives came and went with stiff smiles and sentences that all said the same thing: "This time, it has to be a boy." One daadi even laughed and said, "If it's another girl, just tell her to stop wasting everyone's hopes."

That night, I didn't pray for a brother. I whispered into my pillow, "Let it be a girl. Let her play with us." And when she arrived, tiny, red, and wrinkled, I held her in my lap like a secret the world couldn't steal. My baby sister. Seven pounds of defiance. For the first time, I felt like I had something that truly belonged to me.

But peace was brief. One day, we argued over a broken hair clip. There were shouts, some crying, the usual childish chaos. A neighbour poked her head in and said, loud enough for the whole house to hear, "So much noise; for what? This house is full of girls. Useless girls."

My father heard. He said nothing to her. But later that night, his hand found my cheek. Hard. Unprovoked. Not because of what I did, but because of what she said. Her insult. His shame. My punishment.

I still recall a summer morning when relatives came over. My mother had been up since before dawn, juggling the baby on her hip while rolling out puris, sweat dripping from her forehead. I was maybe six or seven, quietly helping her lay the plates, passing bowls of pickles, and trying not to get in the way. The house was filled with the aroma of fried cumin and hot oil; the kind of aroma that makes guests feel at home. Aunt Rekha, fanning herself with the end of her saree, remarked, "Good; at least she's learning something useful early. That's what makes a girl sanskaari." Chachi Kamla, louder than necessary, added, "Let's hope she doesn't grow up with her nose in books like her cousin. What's the use of education if she can't make perfect rotis?" And Mausi Neela, always the one to twist the knife with a smile, said, "Well, at least this one won't be a burden on her husband's family; she already knows how to serve." Their words weren't meant to wound but to remind us of what girls were expected to be: quiet, capable, marriageable. My mother didn't respond; she just kept moving between the stove and the sink, her face unreadable. I stayed silent, too, though something in me tightened. The work we did was expected, unnoticed, and somehow still not enough.

I stood there holding an empty steel glass, unsure if I was supposed to laugh, too. So I smiled. That's what good girls do; they smile when adults speak, even when something feels wrong. That night, after everyone had left, I lay in bed thinking about that statement. Not because it was new but because it wasn't. Because I knew that no one would correct it. I understood then that some kinds of mistreatment come dressed as ordinary, and that made them harder to fight. That day, something shifted inside me. I didn't have the words for it yet, but I knew I never wanted to be only valid. I wanted to be seen.

The cracks in the house weren't in the walls. They were in the way people stopped talking, in the slammed utensils, in the small fights that left long silences. My mother had started sleeping with the door slightly open, as if even rest had to stay alert. My father came home late and left early. The weight of unmet expectations hovered over every meal.

One evening, there was an argument between my father and grandfather; something about money, something about pride. I don't remember the words. But I remember the sound: a chair scraping back hard, the front door slamming shut, my mother holding my youngest sister too tightly. That night, we ate quietly while the neighbour's TV played someone else's family drama in the background.

A week later, the decision unfolded without ceremony. No one declared it, but the signs were unmistakable. The old trunks were aired out. Sarees were folded with quiet precision. The brass deities were carefully wrapped in yesterday's newspaper. My mother moved through it all with a kind of practised stillness. My father said little, just packed in silence. And I, sensing that questions would only make the silence heavier, kept mine to myself. This wasn't a dramatic exit. It was something softer, sadder; not a fight, but a quiet letting goes. A kind of goodbye that leaves the door open, even as you walk away.

I was ten when we moved out of the joint family home. We relocated near my father's office. The eerie silence followed us like a shadow. My grandmother stopped calling. My grandfather stopped asking about us. My mother grew quieter. Father kept to himself. My sisters and I began speaking in code, using eye signals and half-smiles, as if too many words would break the delicate balance.

Still, I tried to stitch the torn pieces of our family back together. I'd write little notes: "Papa says he misses your upma," "Daadi, we got new bangles",; and tuck them into my father's files, hoping they'd land in the right hands. Maybe words could do what adults couldn't. Perhaps love could be smuggled in through paper.

One and a half years later, my grandfather came back, not with words, not with remorse, but with a small chair for my sister. Bright pink, the kind sold at roadside stalls, its cartoon prints already peeling at the edges. He stood awkwardly at the door, holding it like an offering. No apology or explanation.

We had waited once. For a call, a letter, a knock. But nothing had come. My sister had learned to walk without him, laugh without his lap, and sit on the floor without complaint. And now here he was, with a chair she no longer needed. I took it from his hands, nodded, and placed it by the window. That was his way of saying he still remembered us. It wasn't enough. But it was something. By then, I had changed. I was no longer waiting to be seen. I had begun looking elsewhere, inward.

~

In the village ashram, there were Yagnas held every month. People gathered for rituals and prayers, but I came for the silence. I would sit for hours near the fire, letting the smoke sting my eyes and the warmth steady my breath. I didn't know the mantras. But I felt their weight. I felt seen by the fire in a way I never did by people.

Then, one evening, something happened. I still remember the smell of turmeric in the air and the distant hum of temple bells. I was sitting on the floor at home during prayer when I felt a voice, not outside me, but inside, speak softly:

No more meat. Choose differently.

That night, fish had been prepared. A treat. My favourite once. I looked at my plate and said, "I don't want it."

My mother looked up. "Why?" "I just don't," I said. My uncle chuckled. "Spiritual at eight? What's next, sanyasi at ten?" I didn't respond. I just pushed the plate away. That was the last time I ever sat at a table with meat on it.

It wasn't about the food. It was about listening; not to others, but to myself. That evening, I didn't rebel. I remembered who I was; a young girl is not born to be accepted, but to awaken.

Chapter 2: Away From Home, Closer To Self

"The ache for home lives in all of us. The safe place where we can go as we are and not be questioned."

Maya Angelou, American memoirist and poet

Dreams in my village were always covered in dust, noticeable from afar but fragile up close, easily forgotten as myths were swept away by the breeze. The roads were dry patches of ground smoothed by bullock carts and bare feet rather than paved. They were soaked in the monsoon and cracked in the summer. Our schools weren't "good." We had a single structure with peeling walls and blackboards that bore the scars of time. It was half brick and half hope. Benches tottered and staggered under the weight of growing children. The fan turned unhurriedly and lazily as if it had forgotten why it was made. And the teachers were a steady presence. Some were gentle, others firmer, but all carried a quiet strength. They taught not just from textbooks but from experience, patience, and a deep sense of duty. Even in their silence, there was care. In their presence, we felt the weight of their hopes for us.

We memorised, copied, and obeyed. But inside me, something refused to settle. It wasn't rebellion; it was a question I didn't yet have the words for. A kind of heat rose in my chest when I stared too long at the sky. I didn't know what it meant to crave, but I knew I wanted out of this tired cycle of survival, out of the fate that seemed pre-written. I didn't know where I was headed.

Receiving quality education, especially in villages, was challenging and uncommon. The majority of the kids in my neighbourhood treated school as a way to pass the time until life decided what came next. With government-provided freebies such as uniforms, textbooks, midday meals, and even hostel accommodation for some, it was easier to show up than to stay home. School wasn't always about ambition; sometimes, it was just the more dependable option. But I desired more. I was aware that I would need to earn my way out of the constrained spaces if I wanted to do so, which required passing the Jawahar Navodaya Vidyalaya (JNV) entrance exam, a national exam for students in rural areas. Only a small number of students were chosen from each district, making the selection excessively competitive; however, it provided something unique: a fully residential school that was free of charge, including uniforms, books, food, and everything else.

To prepare and test my luck, I studied using books and hand-me-down guides. I read aloud from passages after supper, worked on maths problems in the morning, and taught myself to maintain discipline even when no one else was around. My name appeared on the list when the results were announced. My destination was JNV, Cuttack. I saw my name linked to a dream for the first time. The school was everything I'd imagined and more: expansive open grounds, clean dormitories, a library filled with books I hadn't even heard of, and students who had come from villages and small towns, just like mine, carrying dreams just as fragile and fierce. Stepping through its gates felt like entering another version of life, one where possibility wasn't just a word but a path. And I had taken my first step.

I packed my bag with hope and dreams and began my life at JNV, Cuttack. It was my first time in a hostel. Everything felt both terrifying and exhilarating. I wasn't sad to leave home. If anything, I felt a strange kind of lightness, like I had slipped out of a skin I'd been wearing too long.

Hostel life was a world governed by bells, charts, and whistles. Days began at 4:30 a.m. with a shrill wake-up call and a blur of white-uniformed students jogging in sleepy unison for physical training (PT). Our beds had to be made with crisp, folded linen. Our rooms were swept clean. After PT, it was a dash to the bathrooms, where cold water was available from shared taps, and buckets jostled under the same rusted spouts. We bathed quickly, dressed quickly, and lined up for breakfast.

Classes ran till lunch, and afternoons were a mix of rest, extra lessons, and doubt-clearing sessions. By 4:00 p.m., the sports field came alive: shouts, whistles, bruises, and laughter. Then came evening studies, dinner at the canteen, and personal time before lights out. We washed our school and sports uniforms with bars of soap that barely lasted a week. Duty rosters rotated our cleaning tasks; from rooms and corridors to classrooms and even the gardens. Navodaya taught us discipline not with fear but with routine. It demanded that we become responsible before we knew what the word meant.

Everything was provided for us: toothbrushes, soaps, notebooks, even blankets and shoes. We didn't have much, but we had equality. In those years, caste, class, and background melted under the same steel plate of dal and rice. We were all just students, all just trying to survive the same schedule, the same homesickness, the same growing up.

Even without a prominent display of privilege, there was an unspoken order, based not on money but on marks. Those who consistently scored well were clearly favoured. Their achievements were quietly celebrated, their presence subtly elevated. For a long time, I didn't try to compete. I wasn't failing, but I wasn't shining either. I understood things, just not fast enough. And slowly, that began to eat at me. I started to wonder if maybe I didn't belong among the brilliant. Maybe my entrance exam success had just been a fluke.

There were four houses in the school: Aravali, Nilgiri, Shivalik, and Udaigiri. I was in Udaigiri. At the time, it meant more than just a name. It felt like belonging to something larger than yourself. That house was a badge of pride, a circle you cheered for, cried with, and competed beside. We screamed ourselves breathless during sports meets, whispered debate lines under our breath before going on stage, and pieced together drama acts with borrowed props and nervous energy. The school never slept quietly. If there wasn't a science congress or a cultural fest happening, we created our reasons to stay up. We sang, rehearsed, argued over who forgot their steps, and turned even the dullest evenings into celebrations. Benches became stages, beds became podiums, and hostel corridors became arenas of creativity and chaos. In those years, we were more than students. We were a patchwork family held together by sleepless nights, inside jokes, shared victories, and the comforting knowledge that even though we were far from home, we had found something close to it.

From Class 6 to 8, I lived like someone who had already arrived; not at the finish line, but at a resting place. Getting into Navodaya had felt like winning something big, and for a while, that win was enough for me. I threw myself into hostel life, enjoying the company of friends, playing games, gossiping under blankets after lights-out, learning songs in the corridor, and laughing until our stomachs hurt during evening snacks. It was the first time I had so much physical and emotional space. No early morning chores, no pressure to top the class, no scoldings waiting at the door. My parents had always been gentle in their expectations. They never asked for report cards with red circles or medals with blue ribbons.

And so, I drifted. I studied enough to pass but never enough to stand out. My notebooks were neat but incomplete. My answers were average. I didn't push, and no one forced me.

But slowly, something swerved.

I noticed that whenever teachers entered the class, they consistently asked the same students to work on problems on the board. When competitions arose, it was always the same names: sharp, polished, and confident. I watched them from my seat at the edge of the third row, smiling like it didn't matter. But it did. I began to feel the quiet weight of being *average*, not because I had failed, but because I wasn't noticed or called first for anything. I wasn't the last, either. Just somewhere in the safe, forgettable middle. That invisibility wasn't loud, but it was persistent. It crept in when I hesitated to raise my hand. It lingered when my name wasn't on any list. I had walked into Navodaya like a spark. But now, I was flickering, not out of light, but out of purpose.

And then, one evening during study hour, something unremarkable happened that I will never forget. A teacher had asked a question; something from math. No one knew the answer, not even the toppers. I did. I didn't raise my hand. I kept it to myself. And when someone else guessed the wrong answer, the teacher moved on. That moment haunted me. Not because I wasn't right, but because I stayed silent when I had something to say.

That night, I sat on the edge of my bunk bed and opened my books, not out of fear or because someone told me to. I did it as I wanted to find my voice again. Quietly, without announcement, I began to change. I started revising regularly. I sat closer to the front. I asked questions. Not many people noticed at first, but I did. I could feel something growing again, not confidence, not yet, but a kind of courage.

In Class 9, everything transformed with one quiet announcement. Our school was sending a few students to another Navodaya in a different state for a year. It was part of a cultural exchange. Ten names would be picked by lottery, and mine was one of them. The classroom buzzed with reactions; some whispered relief, while others expressed sympathy. I stood up, smiled faintly, and nodded like it didn't shake me. But inside, it did. That night, I called home. My father went speechless for a moment, then said, "If this is where you're meant to go, you'll manage." His voice was steady, but I knew him well enough to hear the weight behind it. My mother told me to pack warm clothes. She didn't ask if I was scared. She already knew.

Leaving for Dumka felt like being unplugged from my world. I wasn't just moving schools; I was leaving behind my language, my people, the smells and sounds I didn't know I had memorised. The hostel looked similar, but nothing felt familiar. The taps had no water, so I bought two plastic buckets and made daily trips to the hand pump to collect water. Some days, the food was undercooked and barely edible. But I didn't complain. My father sent ₹500 by money order every month. I used it to buy pens, snacks, toiletries, and almost everything one can think of. But once, due to a postal delay, the money didn't arrive. One month, it didn't come. My purse was empty, and I didn't ask anyone for help. I had one packet of Marie Gold biscuits, just eight pieces. I ate one in the morning and one at night, drank water in between, and waited. I would stand in line every evening asking the warden if the money had come. It hadn't. I went to bed hungry but hopeful. I didn't ask anyone for help. I had learned early that enduring silently was safer than asking loudly.

Then came a moment I had not expected: a game of Kho-Kho. I joined the team, gave it my all, and we won. I was handed ₹260 in cash; my share. That moment didn't change the world, but it changed me in ways I couldn't yet explain. When I held the prize money from the Kho-Kho match, something clicked. I had earned it, not through luck or charity, but through my own effort. I bought food, a pen, and a notebook. Simple things. But I purchased them with pride, and that made all the difference.

That year didn't just teach me how to live alone; it showed me what I was made of. I began to see myself not just as someone who could survive tough days but as someone who could build her answers when no one offered any. Dumka had been difficult; a place of cold meals, dry buckets, and quiet isolation, but it also cracked something open. It showed me a world beyond the narrow paths of my village. A world where people lived differently, spoke differently, and expected differently. And yet, somehow, I found space in it. Although not easily enough to know I could exist outside everything I had ever known.

I missed my parents every day. I remembered my mother's hands in my hair and my father's silence that always said more than words. I held onto those memories like they were light.

When I finally returned to Odisha, I was not the same girl who had left with folded sweaters and nervous eyes. I had seen the "other world"; not the polished one shown on television, but the raw one you walk through with your feet, your hunger, your questions. I had felt a sense of displacement but also the thrill of discovery. I had missed home so profoundly that it ached, but I had also learned how to find comfort in unfamiliar corners. That year taught me the quiet power of adaptation, the invisible strength of choosing to stay when leaving feels easier. It gave me hope, not the soft, dreamy kind, but a sharper one that grows from knowing your resilience. Leaving home hadn't pulled me away from myself. It had brought me closer. I returned with dust on my shoes, a fire in my chest, and the knowing that doesn't need to be spoken. I had found my place in the world, not by seeking it, but by surviving it. And that changed everything.

Chapter 3: Marks Don't Make Me

'Success is not final; failure is not fatal: it is the courage to continue that counts."

Winston Churchill, British Statesman

The summer of 2007 didn't arrive with thoughts of vacations or lazy afternoons eating mangoes. It came with the smell of fresh textbooks, the scratch of pen on paper late into the night, and that heavy, restless feeling you get when the Class 10 board exams are around the corner. Studying for them isn't just about finishing the syllabus; it's about living in a world where every conversation, every meal, even the air in the house seems to revolve around marks. You learn to measure time in chapters completed, not hours passed. I wasn't aiming to be the best in school. I just wanted to see my father's eyes light up with pride and to feel my mother's quiet relief that all her sacrifices had been worth it.

I wasn't just studying for an exam; I was preparing for something I couldn't fully name or explain. Every time I opened my notebook, I didn't dream of ranks or medals. I studied in corners and under murky hostel lights. I memorised formulas when I got time and ran behind teachers with a book in one hand and a dozen doubts in the other. When classmates took breaks, I rewrote notes to learn more quickly. When my body begged for sleep, I whispered out the definitions. As I said, I wasn't aiming for the top but for my parents to say, "She made it."

When the exams ended, I returned home to a routine that felt like a borrowed dream: helping Ma with cupboards, playing with my sisters, eating mangoes in the backyard. I remember telling myself not to expect too much. Just let it be 90%, as that would be enough to make them proud. The day the results were announced, my father kick-started his Hero Honda bike and rode 10 kilometres from his Primary Health Centre to the nearest internet café. That day, nothing could stop him; not the summer heat, not the long road ahead. He just wanted to see my name on that screen. Back then, we didn't have smartphones or Wi-Fi. He handed over my roll number to the café owner, who typed it into a blinking CRT monitor. Minutes later, my father was walking home with a printed sheet in his hand and a stunned expression on his face.

He didn't say anything when he entered. I just stood at the door, breathless, as if the world had shifted. Then he whispered, "Ninety-three point eight per cent." I stared at him. I had to hear it twice. He reiterated it with the same disbelief. "You're the school topper." He was smiling so wide I thought his face would split open. My mother looked at me as if she were trying to hold back tears. My sisters jumped and hugged me, asking what gift I wanted. For a few minutes, time seemed to stand still. The radio in the background crackled with static. The neighbours dropped by when they heard the news. Someone handed my mother sweets. I was still in shock.

Even my teachers were surprised. I had always hovered near the top, but no one saw me as the one to beat. And now here I was, with a score no one expected, carrying a crown I didn't ask for but suddenly had to wear. That day should have felt like an ending. But it felt more like a beginning. Everyone around me celebrated as if it were done. I knew, deep down, that this was just the start of the pressure I had unknowingly invited in.

After my Class 10 results, the world around me narrowed down to one word: The Indian Institute of Technology (IIT). It wasn't just a college. It was a statement; a place that could rewrite the future of an entire family. For students like me, from villages and small towns, getting in felt like being handed a new life. That was when Dakshana happened. Dakshana Foundation is a scholarship-based coaching initiative for academically bright but economically limited students from the Jawahar Navodaya Vidyalayas. Every year, only a select few are chosen. The coaching is complimentary, the quality is privileged, and the promise is straightforward: two years of preparation to crack one of the toughest entrance exams in the country. When I was selected, I didn't celebrate loudly. I felt the weight of what it meant.

For the next two years, my life became unrecognisable. I studied as if my future depended on every test I took. I skipped every distraction; there was no TV, no festivals, and no conversations longer than a few minutes. I stayed up revising, burning the midnight oil. I solved questions until my fingers hurt, for I wanted to prove that a girl from a small district could make it into India's most competitive engineering institute. But when the result came, my name wasn't there. There was no rank or second chance. I refreshed the page, hoping something had glitched. It hadn't. I couldn't speak for hours. I had given everything to this dream; every ounce of effort, every day of my youth, and it still wasn't enough. That failure didn't just break my heart. It made me question who I was without that dream. It felt like the ground had slipped from beneath my feet. I had put all my eggs in one basket, and when it cracked, so did my confidence. For weeks, I went through the motions: eating, speaking, smiling, while carrying a storm inside. It's true what they say: when the heart breaks, it doesn't always make a sound, but you feel the echo in everything you do.

When everything you've used to define yourself, your promise, your potential, your marks, all of a sudden fall apart, what do you do? I had been treating books like sacred treasures for two years, believing that hard work would bring them to me. However, I wasn't merely let down when the sacrifice didn't yield the desired results. I was erased. Exam failure in India causes more than just bruises; it creates a brand. The whispers become more suggestive for a girl. Perhaps this was her breaking point; maybe she should focus on her family responsibilities, take the safe route, or pursue something more "appropriate" for a girl. It was considered as though dreams were too much for her to handle. Thus, for years, I had thought that the solution to everything would be success. But now that no one was clapping, I had to ask myself a more difficult question: Who was I?

In a country where millions of children wake up each day carrying the burden of marks like it's oxygen, failure feels fatal, even when you survive it. The Indian education system doesn't just test your memory; it tests your worth. One number, one rank, and suddenly, your value is up for public auction. I had seen the headlines: toppers celebrated like film stars, and those who didn't make it quietly erased, their names remembered only in condolence messages. Some even chose to disappear completely, unable to bear the shame of facing family, neighbours, or the echo of their unfulfilled dreams. I used to think that happened to "other kids," the ones who were weaker. But that year, I understood. When a dream collapses in a system that treats failure like a curse, even breathing feels like a form of rebellion.

As a girl, I had twice the weight. I wasn't just fighting to prove myself; I was fighting to justify my place in a world already half-convinced that I wasn't enough. Relatives called with rehearsed concern that barely hid their judgment. "It's okay, beta," they said, "IIT isn't for everyone. Maybe now you can focus on getting married?" I laughed politely, but inside, I was sinking. Not because I had failed an exam, but because I felt the world had started to look at me differently — as if I had missed my one shot. I feared I would be seen as "the girl who almost made it," someone who tried too hard, dreamed too big, and ended up back where she started. In that crushing space between who I was and who I wanted to be, I began to lose sight of myself.

I spent days sitting in silence following the heartbreak of missing out on IIT. Even in a crowded house, there is a certain weight to the silence. Although no one held it against me, I could sense a subtle change in the way neighbours enquired and family members spoke, and even my contemplation felt strange after spending two years in a dream that never materialised. It was more than just a rank that was lost. It was as if an identity had been lost. I knew I couldn't stop, though. I applied to state universities using what strength I had left, and I didn't feel like I had won when I received the acceptance letter from Veer Surendra Sai University of Technology (VSSUT). It was similar to breathing, similar to a small thread pulling me forward. It wasn't IIT, but it was mine. A new place, a new start.

On the first day, my father drove me to the university. Thousands of students from low-income families place a high value on VSSUT, one of the most prestigious engineering schools in Odisha. It is frequently a second chance at a first dream and is renowned for turning out engineers who have left their mark at DRDO, Google, and other places. Surrounded by the quiet ambition of hundreds of people, like me, who came with heavy bags and heavier hopes, the campus was situated close to the famous Hirakud Dam. My dad didn't say much. With his love hidden in every little purchase, he subtly bought me notebooks, a mattress, and a bucket. He put my last piece of luggage next to me and said, "Be careful." I couldn't remember who I was anymore as I stared at the ceiling in a hostel bed far from home that night.

However, one thought kept coming back to me: I wasn't done yet. Not just yet. Gradually, VSSUT started to feel more like a silent promise that I could rebuild, this time, according to my terms, rather than just an academic institution.

By the time I entered VSSUT, something in me had changed. I wasn't chasing applause anymore; I was building my rhythm. I chose Electronics and Telecommunication Engineering not for its prestige but because it felt like magic and math had come together. I wanted to understand how invisible waves carried sound and how systems talked to each other. Unlike school, I wasn't worried about standing out. I was more focused on soaking in what I loved. The campus itself felt like a fresh start; lush, calm, and resting near the Hirakud Dam, as if it had all the time in the world. The food was surprisingly good, the hostels manageable, and the academics strong. Labs could have been better, sure, but the air was charged with curiosity. Robotics, innovation, and problem-solving felt like the heartbeat of the place.

In this new space, I slowly carved out my corner. I spent weekends hunched over circuits while others were out watching movies. I said no to distractions and yes to the kind of deep focus that only comes from loving something truly. I formed a small, tight-knit circle of friends who were loyal and still in touch with me to this day, seeing me not as a competitor but as a companion in growth. And somewhere between missed buses, messed-up soldering, and midnight chai, I started rising again. In 2013, I graduated as the branch topper. It didn't come with confetti or cameras. But it brought a quiet satisfaction. A whisper that said, "You didn't need an IIT tag to prove your worth. You did this. On your terms."

After graduation, I was offered a position at a well-known IT firm; it was secure, respectable, and precisely what most students would have taken without hesitation. But something in me resisted. I hadn't spent years falling in love with electronics just to become another face in a cubicle. I wanted more than a job. I wanted to make an impact. So, I made a different choice. I moved to Delhi to prepare for national-level engineering entrance exams, such as the GATE (Graduate Aptitude Test in Engineering) and ESE (Engineering Services Examination), as well as recruitments at BARC (Bhabha Atomic Research Centre), and PSUs (Public Sector Undertakings). Delhi was loud and indifferent, bursting at the seams with ambition and anxiety. The roads never rested, the noise never stopped, and in the middle of it, I carried my dreams in a second-hand suitcase and a notebook full of formulas. It wasn't glamorous, somewhat uncertain, intense, and far from home. But for the first time, I was chasing a future I truly believed in, not for a rank or approval, but for the engineer I knew I could become.

PART II - INTO THE SYSTEM

Chapter 4: The First Rocket I Rode Was Hope

"The future belongs to those who believe in the beauty of their dreams."

Anna Eleanor Roosevelt, American diplomat and activist

After everything I had faced, my IIT heartbreak, the quiet rise at VSSUT, and the long fight to reclaim my confidence, did you think the hardest part was over? No, it wasn't. Life was not easy for me. It was testing me yet again. And this time, the battleground was Delhi.

There was more silence in the room than any rejection when I told my parents that I wanted to move to Delhi for coaching. They were afraid, not because they didn't think I was real. It was shortly after the horrific crime known as the Nirbhaya case, which had destroyed Indian women's sense of safety.

The Nirbhaya case was not just a crime. It was a national wound that refused to close. In December 2012, a young woman boarded a bus in Delhi with her friend, unaware that the journey would become one of the most brutal chapters in the country's recent history. What happened to her shocked the nation and ignited protests in every corner. But more than the public outrage, it changed private lives. Mothers stopped sleeping peacefully. Daughters were called home earlier. Liberty shrank quietly. Delhi became a word spoken with fear. It was no longer just a city; it became a symbol of everything unsafe. For women, the fear seeped into day-to-day choices; what to wear, where to walk, who to trust. Inside homes, fathers hesitated more. Mothers monitored the news with clenched hands. Mothers gripped their daughters more tightly, news outlets played reruns of the footage, and Delhi transformed from a city into a warning.

When I told my parents I wanted to move to Delhi, their silence spoke volumes. It was not that they didn't believe in me. They were terrified of a city that had stolen another girl's future. My mother's eyes filled with quiet dread. My father's pause felt heavier than any lecture. It was my best friend who finally gave them the courage to say yes, promising he would watch over me. That, yes, did not come easily. It carried the weight of fear, faith, and the kind of love that wants to protect but chooses to trust.

Living alone was a sign of defiance rather than ambition for a girl. I saw a quiet fear in my mother's eyes. She didn't say anything, but I knew what it meant. It was the kind of fear many Indian women grow up with, one that doesn't need words. It lives in them, passed down silently from one generation to the next. Usually collected, my father averted his gaze, the corner of his mouth quivering as if he were suppressing all he wanted to say but was unable to. In a society that constantly judges daughters by how quiet they are and how marriageable they seem, my mother made a different choice. She allowed me to chase my dreams. She allowed me to focus on my studies and ambitions rather than succumbing to silence and settling down. When the time came, she handed over her entire savings of ₹85,000 to pay my coaching fees at MadeEasy without a second thought. That act of selflessness became the foundation on which I built my aspirations. It was not only about extending financial support but also her way of telling me that my dreams were worth everything. In that moment, she proved she was not just a mother but a quiet warrior, brave, generous, and fiercely committed to giving me a future she never had. Finally, my best friend made the impossible possible. He assured them that he would assist, check in, and make sure I wouldn't be left alone.

That's when I noticed their tentative nod. Disinclined courageousness, not absolute comfort. It was more than just parental consent at that time. Choosing hope over fear was a sacrifice that only Indian parents of daughters can fully understand.

Delhi moved quickly. People were swarming the streets, chasing time, trends, and metro trains. The campus girls exuded confidence like perfume; they were dressed in the newest styles, their hair was always flawless, and their laughter filled the hallways. I was unaffected by it, though. I didn't come to Delhi to fit in. I wasn't there to draw attention to myself. I was there to win something important but invisible. Every time I closed my eyes, I saw my mother's optimistic silence and my father's weary smile instead of city lights or coffee shops. Every page of my notebook was stitched with the sacrifices they made. I walked past branded stores without blinking, ate the same dal-chawal without criticism, and neglected movie nights and shopping trips; not because I was different, but because I remembered what I was there for. My dreams didn't wear heels or lipstick. They wore urgency. They smelled like ink-stained fingers, early morning air, and the pressure of proving that I belonged; if not to Delhi, then to the future, one I was building test by test.

At MadeEasy, the days blurred into each other like pages of a book I couldn't stop rereading. Mornings began before the city even stirred, and nights ended with my head buried in notes that smelled of ink, sweat, and worry. The PG room was small, with thin walls, but inside, I carried the weight of every expectation. My roommate and I rarely talked about fear, but we knew it sat quietly between us. Sometimes, during chai breaks, I would look at her and say, "Do you think we'll make it?" and she'd shrug, half-smiling, "We have to." I often thought of my best friend back home, the one who convinced my parents to let me come here. In the middle of a long night, when my back ached from hunching over mock tests, I whispered a quiet "thank you" into the dark, hoping somehow, he'd hear it.

Every class at MadeEasy felt like a battle; too many students, too few seconds to grasp complex concepts. I scribbled notes furiously, sometimes copying down entire equations to make sure I didn't miss the method. I signed up for a variety of exams: GATE (Graduate Aptitude Test in Engineering), ESE (Engineering Services Examination), BARC (Bhabha Atomic Research Centre), SAIL (Steel Authority of India), and CEL (Central Electronics Limited), not because I was greedy but because I was scared of being left with nothing. And then, one afternoon, as I sat cross-legged on my bed, too tired to hope, an email popped up from IIT Kanpur. For a few seconds, I couldn't breathe. My hands trembled. I had made it. I was in. The silence in the room wrapped around me like a blanket. I didn't cry. I didn't jump. I just closed my eyes and said, "Finally!"

At IIT Kanpur, I wasn't just stepping onto one of India's top campuses; I was walking into a space that had only recently begun to open its gates to people like me. For decades, only a small number of women were allowed to study. Most of the students were men. As a result, engineering labs often echoed with male voices. As I rolled my suitcase along the lecture halls, that imbalance edged my heart with a quiet tension. I was one of the few girls who belonged here, but I also carried the weight of that new reality. In a place meant to lead the nation, I was living proof that gender barriers could be dismantled with grit, not privilege.

Life here felt electric: the campus buzzed 24/7 with cycles weaving through misty mornings; lights glowed in libraries long after sundown; subsidised cafés served students who lingered late into the night. Peacocks wandered among the lawns, like living reminders that beauty and brilliance could coexist. My stipend of ₹ 8,000 covered food, fees, and hostel; all of it earned, not gifted. It didn't just keep me alive; it nourished a promise I had made to myself and to my parents that I would stand on my own feet.

My daily routine was a blend of lectures, lab work, sports, and job applications. During my second semester, while walking past the lecture halls, I got the call: "You have cleared the ESE written test." My voice cracked as I whispered the news to my roommate. Weeks later, at the UPSC Bhawan in New Delhi and then at the ECoR medical centre in Bhubaneswar, I learned that I was selected for a Space Research company's Ahmedabad centre. I felt it in my bones; a surge of joy mixed with relief. This wasn't just a job offer; it was a career opportunity. It was the culmination of every hour I had poured into dusty exam rooms, every letter home, every silent prayer whispered behind closed doors. I had arrived.

When the job offer finally arrived, it felt like the world had paused for a moment just to let me breathe. I held the letter in my hands and thought of every sleepless night, every tear shed quietly in hostel corridors, every form filled in the face of doubt. It was not just a job. It was the turning point where my years of invisibility finally felt seen. No more roll numbers, no more waiting rooms, no more proving myself through percentages. I was stepping into a role where my work would orbit Earth, where my choices would shape missions and data, not just marks on a map. I was no longer just a daughter chasing dreams; I was becoming a scientist. And somewhere in the back of my mind, I knew this wasn't just my victory. It was for every girl who watched silently from the shadows, wondering if she could do it too.

The move to Ahmedabad came with excitement, yes, but also a quiet sense of responsibility that clung to me like a second skin. My father accompanied me, his very first time on an aeroplane. I remember him peering out of the tiny window with a mix of childlike awe and quiet dignity, the way his fingers gripped the armrest during takeoff, and how his eyes twinkled despite trying to hide it. The first time we stepped out of the Ahmedabad airport, the city felt like a sun-warmed tapestry woven with colour, chaos, and quiet reverence. The air smelled faintly of ghee and incense, and the streets bustled with vendors, auto-rickshaws, and people who all seemed to speak a different rhythm. Bright shops lined the roads, their signs written in looping Gujarati script, and voices echoed greetings of "Jai Shree Krishna" with a warmth that felt ancestral. In Ahmedabad, "Kem cho? Majama!" wasn't just a greeting; it was a reflection of the people's generous hearts. The city was filled with kind, welcoming souls who treated strangers like family and never let a guest leave without tea and snacks. Their laughter was loud, their conversations full of affection, and their doors were always open. Streets bustled with the smell of freshly fried fafda, sweet jalebi, and the familiar voices of vendors who knew their customers by name. During Navratri, every chowk turned into a dance floor, alive with colour and music as neighbours danced together like lifelong friends. On Uttarayan, rooftops overflowed with people sharing food, flying kites, and shouting with joy. The energy of Manek Chowk at night, the calm of the Sabarmati riverfront, and the sacred hush of old temples reflected the many sides of this vibrant city.

It was my father's first time outside Odisha, and I could see him taking it all in: the mustard-yellow buildings, the orderly traffic that somehow made space for the sacred cows, and the surprising peace that lived inside the noise. That evening, before heading to our hotel, we stopped at a small food stall near the Sabarmati riverfront. The vendor handed us paper plates piled high with steaming khaman dhokla; soft, spongy squares of fermented gram flour topped with mustard seeds and coriander. I had never tasted anything like it. It was tangy, sweet, light, and unlike the spice-heavy dishes of home. Ahmedabad introduced itself not just through its roads and people but also through its food, language, and humility. It was a city of contrasts, where glass buildings stood beside century-old temples, and every lane carried a blend of ambition and faith.

We stayed in a modest rented room for a few days as I went through the joining formalities. He followed me from counter to counter, not saying much, just standing tall behind me, as if witnessing the proof that every sacrifice he had made was finally taking form. Soon after, the office gave me a small quarter to stay in. It was simple, with modest rooms and plain furniture. But for me, it felt like a home I had built through years of effort. Each morning, I woke up in silence. There were no bells or classmates, just a peaceful stillness that reminded me I had finally reached a place of my own. Walking to work felt like I was carrying the pride of every setback I had survived. Around me, life was calm. Children cycled to school while neighbours watered plants. I would take it all in and remind myself that I was no longer running toward something but instead living it. My ID card said "Scientist." It didn't just describe a job. It was named after who I had become.

Working at the Premium Research Organisation gave me more than a title. It gave me dignity. It gave meaning to every hour I had studied, every failure I had endured, and every silent tear I had wiped away in hostel corners. The same hands that once carried water buckets in school were now handling data, designs, and research that would one day leave Earth. Some evenings, I would sit at the edge of my bed and take a deep breath. The silence no longer felt empty. It felt earned. My relatives would now speak of me with pride. My father didn't express much, but I noticed the way he listened longer on calls. I knew he kept every article he could find about space and research around the world, proud that I was now part of that field and working for a greater cause. In the dry heat of Ahmedabad, I felt something warmer than the weather. I felt the quiet joy of standing tall in the life I had dreamed about, built on effort, failure, and an unwavering belief that I still had something to give.

Some journeys begin with footsteps, and then some start with belief; raw, trembling, and untaught. Mine was the latter. I didn't have a roadmap, but a resolve. Every closed door, every judgment whispered behind my back, every sleepless night spent holding the weight of two dreams, mine and my sister's, was part of the lift-off. Becoming a scientist was not the peak; it was the proof that women like me, born into modest corners of this country, don't need permission to rise. We build our runways. In a world that often measures women by their silence or sacrifice, I learned to measure myself by my resilience. This wasn't just about launching satellites; it was about redefining gravity itself: the gravity of expectations, fear, and limitations. Perhaps the most beautiful part of the dream was not that I reached it but that I refused to stop believing in it, even when the world tried to tell me I couldn't.

Chapter 5: One Bus, Two Dreams

"There's no greater warrior than a mother protecting her child, and no deeper purpose than love disguised as sacrifice."

Oprah Winfrey, American talk show host

My youngest sister was completing her +2 and nurturing a fierce dream: to become a doctor. She wanted to study in Kota, the mecca for medical aspirants, and though my father was hesitant and worried about safety and distance, I knew we had to take the chance. I convinced him. I took her to Kota, settled her into a girls' PG near Allen Coaching Institute, and bought her everything she might need, from stationery and tiffin boxes to extra bed sheets and warm socks. I paid her coaching fees with my first and second month's salary, in quiet instalments. That salary was my first taste of independence, a symbol of everything I had worked for. But I didn't think twice. We couldn't ask Papa because he still wasn't convinced about sending her to Kota. So I stepped in. That money could have gone toward my own needs, but instead, it went into her dream. And I've never felt prouder. I didn't just leave her there with instructions; I became her second mother, her mentor, and her personal support system. Every fifteen days, I boarded a night bus from Ahmedabad to Kota, navigating fatigue and deadlines to sit across from her, review her notes, motivate her before a test, or simply make her feel less alone. I held my job in one hand and her dreams in the other. She finally cracked the entrance and secured an MBBS seat in a premier government college in Odisha. I cried not the polite tears of happiness but the kind that comes from your gut; the kind that holds every sleepless night, every bus ride, every whispered prayer.

I held her tiny baby fingers the day she was born while the house around us sank into silence because she wasn't a boy. No one said much, but I felt the weight of their unspoken disappointment. That day, I made a silent promise to her. I will love you enough for everyone who won't. I became more than just her sister; I became her second mother. I bathed her, dressed her in soft frocks, slipped lace socks onto her tiny feet, clipped pastel butterflies into her hair, and chose the prettiest accessories to see her smile. I did everything I could to wrap her in the kind of love that shields, uplifts, and says, 'You matter.' Long before she could speak, I was her voice. Long before she could walk, I stood for her. Thus, watching her step into her dream was like reliving mine all over again, only richer and fuller. It made me believe that success isn't just about rising alone but about carrying others upward with you.

There is something I realised about my sister, something that stayed with me long after those Kota days. It's a quality I believe every young woman today can learn from. In an age where it's so easy to get swept up by trends, peer pressure, and the need to keep up constantly, she chose something different. She chose discipline and clarity, and that made all the difference. She never once asked for a new phone. While most girls her age would be excited by a new city, surrounded by fresh air, new faces, and the thrill of freedom, she stayed grounded. In a place where it's easy to get distracted, to follow the crowd, to imitate and absorb everything to feel a sense of belonging, she remained untouched. There was no urge to fit in, no craving to prove anything. While others explored malls and cafes, she clung to her books. While equivalents gave in to pressure and drifted, she dug deeper into her goal. Her world was simple, made up of her dreams, books, and purpose. She used a basic phone, only to call home, never once asking for more. Watching her was humbling. In a time when it's so easy to lose focus, she was indefatigable. It was rare, powerful, and incredibly inspiring.

Dust and untold stories filled the night in Ahmedabad. Wearing the same pale-blue cotton kurta that I had worn to work that morning, with the collar still stiff from the memory of science labs and solemnity, I stood at the edge of the packed bus stop. My hair was tied in a loose plait, and I carried a small leather bag over my shoulder that contained a notebook, my sister's test printouts, medications, and a half-empty bottle of water. Around me, the city was bustling with the usual commotion: cars honking, vendors shouting, the smell of fafda and Kesari jalebis, and the damp earth from prolonged water sprays. Ahmedabad was gradually influencing me, not only through the Gujarati words I was beginning to understand or the dhokla's flavour that no longer shocked me, but also through the way I started to move; quietly and effectively, just like the city itself.

I wasn't just a professional on vacation when I boarded the bus headed for Kota. I was someone else, a guardian, a sister, a bearer of borrowed hope. I had grown accustomed to sitting by the window. I found solace in the frayed fabric. I followed the haze of traffic lights as they transformed into stars. Passengers around me fell asleep or whispered into their phones, but I remained alert. I had learned by then that some journeys aren't for rest. They're for remembering why you started. My sister had a dream; to heal and to serve; and I'd promised myself I'd help her reach it. Each journey was more than a trip. It was a quiet act of rebellion against the idea that women must rise alone. That bus didn't just carry me from Ahmedabad to Kota; it had two dreams. And mine, that night, was dressed in a faded kurta and unwavering purpose.

Taking on the role of a mother while still learning to stand tall myself was never part of the plan, but love often writes its script. With our mother far away and my sister facing the pressure of becoming a doctor, I stepped into a space that required more than money or logistics; it needed presence. I became the one who reminded her to eat, who tucked her in with late-night calls before a test, who decoded test analysis like lullabies. I wasn't just checking her notes; I was reading her silences, sensing her fear, catching her when she stumbled between hope and exhaustion. Our bond transformed in those long months. We weren't just sisters anymore. I became her shadow in the daylight and her strength after dark, someone who absorbed her stress so she could sleep more easily. And in doing that, I discovered how deeply love can root itself in action.

The experience shaped her as much as it changed me. Watching me juggle work, buses, and her dreams lit something in her; a quiet fire of gratitude that bloomed into resilience. She began to see discipline not as pressure but as love. She studied not out of fear but out of a sense of purpose. I watched her posture straighten, her eyes steady. Her self-doubt gave way to determination. "If you can do so much for me," she once whispered, "how can I not show up for myself?" That moment cracked something open in both of us. It reminded me that nurturing someone's ambition isn't about grand gestures; it's in the tiffin packed with care, the notes reviewed late into the night, and the unwavering belief that their wings will take flight. Her journey to MBBS was not walked alone. It was built on our bond; sisterhood as a shared courage, mothering as an act of sisterly love.

Once her coaching was over, we entered the most critical phase of her journey. We began applying for every major medical entrance exam in the country. We filled out forms for NEET (National

Eligibility cum Entrance Test), AIIMS (All India Institute of Medical Sciences entrance exam), and JIPMER (Jawaharlal Institute of Postgraduate Medical Education and Research entrance exam), among others. They are among the toughest competitive exams in India, with lakhs of students appearing each year, all competing for a limited number of seats in top medical colleges. The level of pressure and practice required is inconceivable unless you experience it firsthand.

I took the duty of handling every detail, from reading the fine print to collecting documents, keeping track of dates, and ensuring everything was done perfectly. Like a guardian, I accompanied her to every examination centre, whether it was in Ahmedabad or Gandhinagar. On the morning of each exam, I packed her belongings, carried her admit card as if it were gold, and ensured she arrived with a relaxed and attentive mind. While she went in to fight her battle, I waited outside in the blistering heat for three or four hours, shrouded by dozens of equally apprehensive parents. The sun charred my skin, but I never moved. I had made a promise to my parents that I would not let her fail, not because she lacked proficiency but because her dream had become my mission. And I was inclined to do whatever it took to see it come true.

Managing a full-time job at the Space Research company while boosting someone else's endeavour wasn't a balancing act; it was a daily tightrope walk without a safety net. My days began before sunrise and ended long after the world had fallen asleep. In the lab, I worked on research problems that required a sharp focus. But even between simulations and project reviews, my mind often drifted to Kota; had she eaten? Was her test score bothering her? Did the PG have a water supply that day? I had spreadsheets on one screen and her test schedule on another. I crammed in grocery runs between deadlines, stood in queues for couriering her books, and took calls hiding in stairwells to reassure her that things would be okay. It was messy and often invisible. But this was the unrecognised work that mothers, mentors, and sisters have done quietly for generations, turning chaos into consistency so that someone else could fly.

There were weeks when my body gave up before my will did. The night buses left me with a sore back and dry eyes. I skipped social events, declined promotions, and postponed personal joys, not because I was selfless but because I had made a choice. It is a deliberate, exhausting, beautiful choice. To care. To show up. To believe that dreams built for two are heavier, yes, but also more meaningful. There were evenings I cried alone, not from sadness but from the fatigue of carrying more than one life at a time. Yet I never questioned it because in doing so, I wasn't just helping her become a doctor; I was constructing a future where women don't have to choose between ambition and love, between nurturing others and achieving for themselves. This was my sacrifice, yes, but also my noiseless revolution.

Sacrifice, I've come to believe, is not always loud or glorious. It often slips in quietly, like steam from a chai cup, rising, disappearing, and leaving behind only warmth for those who notice. Some sacrifices melt away like ice cream on a summer day, gone before anyone remembers what it cost. But others are like gold. Not flashy or loud, but enduring. They stay, collecting memories, meaning, and weight over time. What I gave during those months, from the late-night buses to the skipped meals, the unread books on my nightstand, and the calls to her hostel after long hours at the lab, wasn't just a to-do list. It was love folded into a schedule. It was faith disguised as routine.

When I look back now, I don't remember every detail of the exhaustion. I recall how her voice shifted from hesitation to conviction. I remember the way she started sitting up straighter and speaking more clearly. I remember the day she said, "You didn't let me give up, so how could I?" And in that moment, I understood that this wasn't just about helping someone crack an entrance exam. It was about rewriting what sisterhood could mean. I wasn't just her guardian. I was planting courage where fear had lived and discipline where doubt had grown.

No, I don't have medals for those months, nor do I have headlines or ceremonies. But I have something far richer; a bond burnished by struggle, a story etched in night rides and whispered affirmations. And like heirloom gold, it shines in places no one else can see but us.

PART II - INTO THE SYSTEM

Chapter 6: The Line I Drew

"Sometimes in life, you have to fight even with yourself. And to win, all you need is courage.

Sudha Murty, Indian author, philanthropist, and educator

Motherhood changed my life by redefining it. It held up a mirror I hadn't expected and asked me to recognise myself anew. Long before I ever cradled my baby, I had been harbouring the imperceptible weight of identities I had never chosen thoroughly. I was the daughter who kept quiet, the wife who adjusted, the daughter-in-law who obeyed, and the employee who over-delivered. Each role asked me to adapt myself to smaller renditions so that others could feel comfortable. And for years, I did it without protest.

But when I became a mother, something in me refused to keep folding. It was not just my child who was born. A woman was born, one who had no tolerance left for quiet suffering, one who could no longer nod and agree while her body ached and her heart screamed. In those early hours of postpartum pain, with milk-stained nights and a body that felt foreign, I realised I was unravelling. But this unravelling was not a failure. It was an awakening.

No one teaches you that motherhood will confront your soul. While everyone is watching the baby, no one sees the mother breaking open in silence. People surrounded me, yet I still felt invisible. I had given birth, yes, but now I had to give birth to a voice that had been buried beneath years of being polite. That voice rose slowly, not in anger but in truth. It whispered, "You matter too." It reminded me that sacrifice without self-respect is not devotion; it is disappearance. This was the beginning of my becoming. And for the first time in my life, I was not ashamed to say it aloud; I will not lose myself to please others. I will not say yes when my body, my heart, and my truth say no. I had entered motherhood believing I had to give everything. But I stayed in motherhood by learning to give to myself first. It's like the safety instructions on a plane, where the air hostess says: ' Put your oxygen mask on first before helping others. ' I used to think that was selfish. Now I see it's survival. You can't pour from an empty cup, and you can't breathe life into others if you're gasping for air yourself. And like the flight attendant says, secure your life jacket before assisting anyone else. That simple instruction carries the weight of a truth I had to learn the hard way: saving yourself isn't neglect; it's the first act of genuine care, not just for you but for everyone who depends on you. I wasn't stepping away from motherhood. I was stepping into it more fully, with strength rooted not in exhaustion but in self-respect and presence.

Near my house stands a great banyan tree. Its wide, outstretched branches offer shade to birds who protect themselves from rain and harsh weather. Animals rest beneath it, and people pause under its cool, generous canopy. It gives without asking, but only because it stands tall and whole itself. Had it not grown strong, had it not branched out with courage and rooted itself deep into the earth, it could not offer what it does. If it had been frail or slanted like a creeping vine, clinging and dependent, it wouldn't have become the shelter it now is. Its strength is in itself while acting as a refuge for others. In many ways, that is how I now see myself: I cannot become a source of comfort or support unless I first stand in my strength, rooted and whole.

I remember one morning, just two weeks after giving birth, standing in the kitchen to prepare breakfast while my body ached and my baby cried softly in the other room. My stitches were still painful, and I had barely slept. Yet I found myself moving through the familiar motions of routine. At the time, no one questioned why I was out of bed, and I now understand that their response was not due to a lack of care. It came from deeply rooted traditions and belief systems were returning to normalcy quickly was seen as a sign of strength and responsibility. In many households, especially in earlier generations, care was often expressed through structure, through fulfilling one's role quietly and without complaint. These actions were shaped by what people believed was right and by what they had experienced themselves. As I stirred the dal with shaky hands and a tired smile, I did not feel anger but rather sensed the beginning of a quiet realisation. Later, while feeding my baby in the stillness of the afternoon, I told myself that it was time to listen to my own body. It was time to begin expressing what I needed, not in opposition to tradition, but more as an act of understanding myself more fully within it.

That night, I tried to bring it up gently with my husband. I said, "I'm not okay. I need help." He looked uncomfortable, then replied, "Everyone is tired in the beginning. It will get better." His words, though not unkind, felt like a door closing on my distress. I wanted to scream, "It's not just tiredness. It's drowning." But I didn't. I nodded and turned away. Inside, a small fire started to burn.

It's strange how quickly the mother disappears behind the baby. The congratulations pour in, but the concern rarely reaches her. Postpartum depression does not arrive with warning signs or ceremony. It slips in quietly, hiding behind forced smiles and the weight of unspoken expectations. It is a silence soaked in shame.

We are expected to rejoice, not struggle. Mental health is barely whispered about, and a mother saying she is not okay is often met with dismissiveness or disbelief. When I tried expressing my overwhelm, someone said, "Sabke saath hota hai. Tumhari maa ne bhi jhela tha." That sentence hit me like a slap. Just because pain is common, does that mean it should be ignored? Why do we celebrate motherhood but often forget the mother?

In India, postpartum depression is frequently labelled as seasonal mood changes or emotional overreaction. In truth, it is a serious mental health issue that requires compassion and proper assistance. Countless women suffer from this condition because they feel the need to maintain a façade of happiness while, in reality, they are dealing with immense strain due to physical pain, emotional turmoil, pain cloaked behind societal expectations, and much more. This is not a phase; rather, this period is critical within the mother-infant bond attachment system, which, if neglected, could lead to negative long-term consequences for a woman's well-being, particularly her self-image, mothering ability, and bonding with her child across decades. The implications are multifaceted, encompassing alterations to one's emotions, as well as the domains of neurology and hormones, which form deeply interdependent connections often defined as relational systems.

In nations like Japan, this shift is approached with great thoughtfulness. Mothers benefit from extended paid maternity leave, along with comprehensive home nurse visits, mental health screenings, and access to postnatal recuperative facilities that support the integration of mother-child wellness. Such actions are not optional; they emerge from scientific study and deep compassion and admiration for what a woman goes through during and after pregnancy. Conversely, many households in

India expect mothers who have recently given birth to immediately start fulfilling domestic responsibilities, which reflects cultural norms that are out of touch with reality.

Postpartum depression is often disregarded, but it requires immediate attention and action. Any society willing to bear witness to the miracle of life being gifted must also be prepared to offer extensive support enabling the woman carrying the child to walk through her life's most challenging phase safely. The emotional well-being of a mother is by no means a footnote in the childbearing narrative – it is a central part of it. If pain continues to receive unaddressed acknowledgement alongside an overlooked drawing board, generations will drown in an ocean of muted agony.

Supporting mothers is not a gesture of kindness. It is a responsibility. One that determines the emotional climate of families, communities, and the future itself. The question is not whether we care but whether we are willing to care in the ways that truly matter.

Setting boundaries was not an act of rebellion. It was an act of survival. I began speaking up, often quietly, sometimes shakily, but with growing clarity. I told my husband what I needed, not with bitterness, but with truth. I told my in-laws where I stood, not with anger, but with firmness. I allowed myself to feel guilt, and then I let it go. For the first time in my life, I said no and meant it.

It did not happen overnight. Boundaries were met with resistance. There were questions, whispered judgments, and cold silences. I was told I had changed. I was told I was becoming too sensitive. But what they did not understand was that I had finally learned the cost of saying yes to everything. I had finally seen how a woman could lose her identity one polite nod at a time. And I was no longer willing to lose myself.

One evening, I sat on the bathroom floor, the only space where I could cry in private. My baby had been crying nonstop. My mother-in-law was voicing her disapproval of me for being "too soft," and my husband was silent, stuck between loyalty and logic. My thoughts raced like an untamed river: “Am I failing? Am I the only one who feels this miserable? Why can’t anyone see I need help?” That night, I wiped my tears and made a decision. I was done pretending.

I began to reclaim the parts of me I had shelved. I started journaling again. I carved out time to read. I stepped outside with my child, not to escape but to breathe. I allowed myself to be more than someone who gets things done. I chose to become someone who feels, who pauses, who lives.

Motherhood does not end your identity. But it will erase it if you are not paying attention. I learned this the hard way. Everyone discussed the baby’s sleep cycles, feeding schedules, and weight milestones. No one spoke about the mother’s emotional chaos, the mental clutter, the sheer loneliness that crept in even when the room was packed.

Balancing extended family and motherhood felt like walking a tightrope on a windy day. My time was no longer my own, yet I was expected to smile, serve, and stay silent. I realised I had internalised a great deal of this. I was saying yes before I was even asked. But not anymore. The shift was not loud, but it was final. I was not angry. I was just done, done with pleasing, proving, and waiting for someone to notice I was drowning.

I started redefining respect. Respect was not keeping quiet when I was hurting. It was not bending to keep the peace. Respect, I learned, begins within. When I respect myself enough to say no, others may not clap, but they learn where the line is. And that line? That is where my dignity lives.

There were days when I faltered, days when the guilt returned like a shadow at dusk. When I wondered if I was being too rigid, those moments passed. Because the woman I was becoming was no longer ruled by guilt. She was led by clarity. I was not abandoning my family. I was coming home to myself.

I also learned that balance does not mean everything is equal. It means everything is intentional. Some days, I chose my child over a social obligation. Some days, I decided that my mental peace was worth a festival gathering. Some days, I decided to rest while others expected me to entertain. And in doing so, I found a strange kind of strength. Not the type that shouts, but the kind that stays steady like a lighthouse in a storm.

I stopped explaining my choices. I started trusting them. I stopped trying to be the version of a woman that made everyone else comfortable. I began to become the version of myself that allowed me to breathe. Slowly, I began to feel proud; not just as a mother, but as a woman who had taken her place in the world, one quiet boundary at a time.

In the quiet moments between my baby's sleep and the world's noise, I began to observe the rhythms of nature more closely. A tree does not apologise for needing both rain and sunlight. A river does not explain its changing pace. Birds leave the nest when it is time; not out of rebellion, but because it is part of their becoming. I began to realise that motherhood, like nature, is not about perfection. It is about presence, adapting, surrendering, and still claiming expanse to grow. Watching the morning sun pour over my balcony or feeling the softness of the earth under my feet reminded me that I, too, am allowed to be cyclical, raw, and real. I am not meant to bloom for others endlessly. I am meant to rest, to feel, to break, and to begin again.

Motherhood gave me many things, but most of all, it gave me back to myself. Not in the way I once was, but in a way I had never dared to be. I carry invisible scars, not just from surgery but from years of silencing my own needs. And yet, those scars are not wounds anymore; they are proof that I have lived, endured, and transformed. I have learned to listen when I am tired. I have learned to speak even when my voice shakes.

And most importantly, I have learned that a woman who honours her truth teaches her children to do the same. This is not the ending of a chapter but the rooting of something more profound, something firm and quiet and full of grace.

This chapter of my life has no dramatic ending. It ends with a line, a line I drew gently, firmly, and finally. A line that says, 'I matter too.' A line that does not isolate me from others but connects me to myself. And in that connection, I found something I had lost along the way: my courage, clarity, and identity.

From that day forward, I began living with one quiet promise: No more yeses.

PART III - THE EMOTIONAL UNDERCURRENT

Chapter 7: Motherhood: The Version No One Told Me

"I had to stand up for myself. Because if I didn't, no one else would."

Kiran Bedi, 24th Lieutenant Governor of Puducherry, India

Marriage, in our culture, is not merely the union of two people; it is a construct layered with expectations, especially for a woman. The moment sindoor (vermillion) is applied, another role begins to take shape in the minds of others: that of a mother. From parents and in-laws to curious neighbours and even strangers, the question inevitably follows: "When are you going to have a baby?"

For us, though, there was no such pressure. My husband and I had no immediate plans to start a family. We were content in our new life together, focusing on building our relationship and navigating the early days of marriage.

Motherhood was never something I pictured for myself. I was busy figuring out who I was, learning new things, and creating a life that felt like mine. I didn't disregard the idea of having kids; it didn't fit into my plans at the time. But then, something began to change. I started to imagine becoming a mother; it was a subtle thought that crept in without any urgency. It just lingered softly, showing up in quiet moments when I least expected it.

During the COVID-19 lockdown, everything shifted dramatically. I found out I was pregnant, and it completely took me by surprise. My initial reaction was a mix of shock and a whirlwind of questions. However, as we reflected on the news and discussed it, I began to find some peace with the idea. We decided to go ahead and have the baby, and it wasn't a choice made out of fear or pressure. Instead, it came from a place of love and hope, an instinct that maybe this unexpected change was meant to lead us to something extraordinary.

The next morning, we went to the hospital to be sure. The air smelled of sanitiser and quiet tension. Though it was a private maternity hospital, it felt as busy as a train station. Fathers paced nervously, elderly parents sat praying, and expectant mothers waited with rounded bellies and tired eyes. A woman in labour passed by in a wheelchair, her mother clutching a bag and trembling beside her. A toddler ran down the hallway while his pregnant mother rubbed her back and smiled faintly. On the walls were photos of newborns with welcome signs. I stared at them, wondering what our child might look like. A childbirth awareness video played on a screen, but no one was watching. Everyone was lost in their own waiting.

When our turn came, my heartbeat thundered in my ears. The doctor was calm and kind, listening as I explained my symptoms. She outlined the following steps: blood tests to check for the pregnancy hormone, one to confirm its presence, and the other to measure how far along I might be. I nodded as if composed, but inside, my thoughts raced. The hallway to the lab felt unusually long. It smelled like spirit and floor polish. The nurse, in a crisp white uniform, handed me the slip with a warm smile as if she already knew what was coming. After the blood test, the doctor recommended an early ultrasound scan to confirm the pregnancy visually.

After completing the tests, we returned home. About two weeks later, the hospital called and asked us to come and collect the reports. We were back in the doctor's cabin. We sat with our fingers tightly intertwined. The gynaecologist looked at the results, then looked up and smiled. "Congratulations," she said. "You're pregnant."

The world was still full of fear. COVID-19 was everywhere. Vaccines had just started, and no one knew if they were safe for pregnant women. The doctor asked us if we wanted to continue. It was a difficult question. We spent days thinking, talking, and attempting to comprehend what was right. Ultimately, we decided to move forward, trusting our instincts.

In those nine months, each trimester carried its rhythm and emotion. The early weeks were filled with anticipation, but also brought intense nausea that made eating complex and even simple tasks like brushing my teeth feel impossible. Fatigue settled around me like a shawl, and yet, I found a quiet comfort in knowing that my body was creating life. As I entered the second trimester, I felt a sense of relief. My energy slowly returned, and I experienced moments of calm and lightness. The baby's first movements felt like soft flutters, a secret only I could feel. I began to enjoy preparing meals, taking gentle walks, and imagining names, lullabies, and the kind of mother I might become. People often told me I looked like I was glowing, but they could not see the quiet waves of emotion moving through me. There were nights I lay awake, wondering how I would face labour and whether I was truly ready for all the changes ahead. During the last trimester, my body grew heavier with each passing day. Sleep became uncomfortable, my back ached constantly, and even small tasks required great effort. Yet, through all of this, each kick and nudge made me feel more deeply connected to the little soul inside me. I'd sit quietly, savouring pieces of chocolate and sweets, each bite sweeter with the thought of my baby growing inside me. As I ate, I'd speak softly to my little one, play temperate music, and smile at every tiny kick and flutter. Those moments felt sacred, just the two of us sharing silent conversations long before we finally met.

There were difficult moments, which included mood swings, bloating, swollen feet, and sudden frustration. Yet, beneath it all, I felt a sense of awe at how my body quietly endured and adapted. I began to trust in a deeper, resilient part of myself, turning to prayer and learning to let go. Those months became less about waiting for my baby and more about meeting a new, stronger version of myself.

Pregnancy during the pandemic was full of surprises. The world outside shut down, but inside me, the world was coming to life. Every kick, flutter, excitement, and fear marked it. There were no baby showers, gatherings of loved ones, and extended visits from friends and family. Instead, there were masks, solitude, and strategically scheduled visits to prevent large gatherings of people. I was nurturing life in my womb while living in a world that was gearing up for death.

The pandemic brought with it a heaviness that not only surrounded me but also slowly made its way into the deepest parts of my being. Emotionally, I began to unravel. Each day felt like moving through a fog, where joy had lost its voice, and hope had become a whisper I could barely hear. Isolation crept in quietly at first, then all at once. No one could travel. The people who would hold my hand, comfort me, or even sit beside me in silence were all locked away, separated by distance, fear, and the brutal uncertainty of a pandemic. In the middle of all this, my dearest friend, someone whose dreams of motherhood once mirrored mine, was also pregnant. She was seven months pregnant, living in a remote village with limited access to proper medical care.

We would speak often, and she told me about the loneliness that filled her days, the silence in her home, and how pregnancy, which should have been joyful, now felt like a long road walked alone. She was unable to travel due to strict restrictions. But she was cautious and followed every guideline. But none of it was enough. When she told me she had tested positive for COVID-19, I remember feeling a chill in my bones. Then, days later, I heard she had a miscarriage. And soon after, she too passed away. I still remember sitting down on the cold floor, one hand on my belly, the other covering my mouth as if trying to contain a scream that was never meant to be silent. I wept until my body gave way to exhaustion. Her death shattered something in me. She had always been my reflection, and suddenly, that reflection was gone. I thought of her last moments, alone, scared, and with no one to console her. I whispered her name into the darkness at night, hoping she could somehow hear me. Her absence was everywhere. It followed me into every checkup, every ultrasound, and every hopeful moment, now met with caution. I could not sleep or breathe without the ache of missing her. That loss took root in me, becoming a silent shadow I carried into motherhood. It changed how I felt about my pregnancy and altered my perspective on the world. And though I did not know it at the time, it became the beginning of something much weightier, the modest unravelling of my mind and heart that would later become postpartum depression. But in those early days, it was just pain that was wordless, wild, and impossible to run away from.

Hope didn't arrive easily, but we treated it like something to be nurtured and cultivated. I began writing letters to my baby, simple words filled with love and promise. I filled notebooks with thoughts, trying to let the worry pass through ink instead of holding it inside. Some days, I would find comfort in folding tiny clothes and organising baby things with quiet intention. We lit candles in the evenings, shared stories that made us laugh, and reminded ourselves that we were getting through this together. It was in these small, steady acts that hope found its place.

Each hospital trip was like trespassing behind enemy lines. I double-checked the papers, the scripts, and the sanitiser stashed in my bag, all the while silently hoping that neither I nor my unborn baby would touch the virus. The sonography room, where magic and first impressions were once made, was now sterile and cold behind misty face shields. And all the while, my husband tried to be there for me, but there were boundaries to what he could see, feel, or comprehend.

And then came the day. I had prayed for a normal delivery, something peaceful and lovely. But destiny had other ideas. Labour complications accelerated rapidly, and I was wheeled into the operating theatre for an emergency C-section. Harsh lights above, the air surprisingly sterilised, and masked faces all around me, whose eyes were the sole visible sign of emotion. When anaesthesia began numbing my body, my mind went into a wild spin: Was my baby safe? Was I going to be alright? Would someone be waiting outside? Would I feel like a mother when this was all over?

Then, in the cold clatter of instruments and muffled speech, I heard it: a cry. Tears streamed down the sides of my face. I had not yet seen him, but that cry told me that he was here. Safe. Breathing. Alive. I wanted to hold him, to say to him that I was his mother, but my arms remained frozen. My body remained numb, but my heart, my heart ached with it all. As I lay there on the operating table, numb from the anaesthesia, I kept looking toward the nurses and doctors for some signal.

I had heard his cry, but I needed confirmation. My mind was spinning with questions I couldn't speak out loud. Was he okay? Was he breathing well? Were all his vitals in range? After what felt like hours compressed into seconds, a nurse finally turned to me and said, "He's stable. Everything is normal." At that moment, a weight I didn't even know I was carrying lifted from my chest. I felt an overwhelming sense of relief flood my body. My child was safe. That one sentence anchored me amid all the chaos. The most challenging part was done. But I was about to discover that giving birth was merely the start of an infinitely more profound, lonely fight.

Recovery from the surgery was torturous. The pain and emotional strain left me unable to care for my baby the way I had longed to. Watching my little one cry in hunger while I lay helpless was heartbreaking, and those moments left an ache deeper than the physical wounds. My heart hurt each time the nurses approached with a bottle rather than encouraging skin-to-skin contact. I needed compassion and care. But what I got was the expectation, an expectation that was not spoken, that I would "bounce back," as if an extensive abdominal surgery and the emotional burden of being a new mom did not matter. My mother-in-law visited during this period. A woman of strength, undoubtedly, but a woman of a different generation, one where it is believed that silence is strength and hardship is a virtue. I could not be this woman. I was falling apart. I could not eat. I bled and seethed. I was alone.

~

In the days that followed, something subtle changed between my husband and me. I could tell he wanted to help, and I noticed it in the way he looked at me and how he hovered nearby, trying to be supportive but unsure of what to do. I understood he was trying, but I didn't have the energy to show him what I needed. I felt overwhelmed, physically sore, and emotionally drained, which made it hard to ask for support. While he seemed helpless in the face of my pain, I kept my struggles to myself. This created a quiet distance between us. I didn't blame him; I knew he meant well. I started to carry my emotional burdens alone, unsure if I could rely on anyone else. Within me, things began to shift gradually. I created a little space where I could be vulnerable without having to explain myself. I didn't talk about it, but I put up a gentle boundary. What had once felt easy and close between us began to feel uncertain. I missed our connection, but I couldn't figure out how to rekindle it. Perhaps this is one of the hidden truths of early motherhood. It doesn't only reshape your body and your days. It also rearranges your relationships, often without your awareness. And in those early moments, I learned how to be there for myself when everything around me felt unsure.

The days ahead were grey. I despised the baby I had nurtured so tenderly for nine months. I loathed the crying, the dependency, the constant exhaustion. I abhorred the way people doted over the baby, and I was invisible. The more I required assistance, the lonelier I became. Without maternal support, I was unable to travel because of the pandemic, and without professional guidance, I lapsed into a state of numbness, into postpartum depression.

Postpartum depression is not something that is talked about in Indian households. It is often brushed aside as weakness, moodiness, or unnecessary drama. But what I experienced was real and all-consuming. I was not simply tired or overwhelmed. I felt as though I was sinking into a darkness I could not describe. Each day felt heavy, as if I were moving through the thick fog that dulled every sensation. I became short-tempered, easily irritated, and so deeply exhausted that even basic tasks felt impossible. Feeding my baby, getting out of bed, brushing my hair; everything required an effort I did not have. I cried often, sometimes for no reason, and felt an unbearable guilt for not feeling the joy I had expected. When I looked at my baby, there were moments I felt nothing at all, and that emptiness frightened me more than anything else. My body had started to heal, but my mind felt broken, distant, unreachable. I kept hoping I would return to myself, that this feeling would pass, but the days only grew heavier. Postpartum depression was not a passing sadness. It was a deep, unspoken ache that consumed my thoughts, made me question my worth as a mother, and left me feeling isolated in a world that expected me to glow.

When we shifted to our hometown in Odisha, I had expected to improve with the fresh air and familiarity. But the sleepless nights persisted. Without house help, I was finding it difficult to manage household work, vaccination schedules, and baby care. Yet, gradually, my son began to bond with me. His babbling, his sleepy smile, and his little fingers holding mine started rebuilding the bridge between us. I began to forgive myself for the emotions I had felt. I started realising that depression did not make me a bad mother. Instead, it made me human. And that's when the actual transformation occurred. I said to myself, 'This is over.'

There were moments in the early days when I looked at my child and felt nothing but resentment. His cries cut through my exhaustion. His constant needs overwhelmed my aching body. I began to feel trapped in a role I had once waited for with so much hope. I hated the silence during breastfeeding. I hated the endless sleepless nights. And more than anything, I hated the version of myself that was emerging. I was angry, impatient, and emotionally distant. With that hatred came an unbearable sense of guilt. What kind of mother feels this way? What type of woman resents her baby? I carried that shame quietly, unable to speak it out loud. I flinched when others called him a blessing because I could not yet feel it. But healing began, slowly and silently. It came in the way his warm breath rested against my skin, in the way his fingers wrapped around mine without expectation. I began to understand that he was not the cause of my pain. He was only a baby. I was the one hurting. And in that realisation, something softened. Tenderness found its way in. Guilt slowly turned into forgiveness.

I started to see him, truly see him, and from that space of quiet understanding, love began to grow. Not loud or perfect, but real. This version of motherhood was nothing like what I had imagined. It was not the one wrapped in lullabies and pastel-coloured blankets. It was the one filled with blood, silence, aching, and invisible battles. No one had told me that I might feel hatred before love or guilt before grace. No one said to me that I could feel both joy and resentment in the same breath. But I have lived through it. And now I know that this version, my version, is valid too. It may not be picture-perfect, but it is painfully honest, deeply human, and worth telling.

Chapter 8: Quiet Pillars, Loud Love

"The family is one of nature's masterpieces."

George Santayana, Spanish-American philosopher

Family in India is not just a blood bond. It is a spiritual thread of generations, a vital force that determines who we are from the moment of birth. It is our first identity, our refuge in times of trouble, and our pride in times of triumph. In Indian houses, family is not just parents and children. It spills over into common courtyards, where grandparents, uncles, aunts, cousins, and even neighbours become like family. It is in how a mother sets aside the best bite of food for her child without uttering a word and in how a father stands quietly in the background, fighting his fatigue to provide for the family's needs. We are raised in tales told by grandmothers under mosquito nets, in lullabies sung in dying dialects, and in festivals that put everyone on the same prayer mat or floor mat. We are raised not only with recipes and rituals but also with values such as respect, duty, and sacrifice. In each Indian household, love is often shown more in deeds than in words. It is seen in the form of a father waking up early to get milk before the line is formed, or a sister waiting for her brother to return before having her meal.

Even in adversity, family is a source of enduring strength. Where one falters, others support him. Where one has dreams, others have faith. It is not uncommon in our civilisation for parents to sacrifice their comforts so that their children may study, relocate to unfamiliar towns, or endure society's scorn in silence for the sake of household harmony. In Indian families, women have long been the unobtrusive pillars of family strength above all. They keep secrets in their silence and strength in their drudgery. As we age, we realise that family is not where we are from but what continues through us. It is the voice within us that directs us. It is the scent of a mother's massage oil, the act of bowing to touch the feet of elders when we leave the house and the comfort of being called by our childhood name. In this nation, where human beings take precedence over money, where roots come before wings, family is not a part of life; rather, it is life itself.

In every family, some people speak loudly, while others are a quiet yet powerful force. I come from a family of women whose resilience was never shouted. It showed up in perseverance, in renunciation, and in the kind of love that didn't ask for recognition. We were not raised to say, "Look at me." We were raised to say, "I'm here. I will carry it with you."

My mother never gave extravagant lectures about courage. She lived it every single day. She was the youngest of nine siblings and lost her father when she was just ten years old. Despite excelling in her studies, particularly in English and Maths, she never had the opportunity to complete her education. Fear, family pressure, and duty pulled her away from the classroom and into a life she didn't choose, but never turned her back on. She moved into a relative's home, immersed herself in domestic life, and years later, married a man she had met only on her wedding day: my father.

What followed were years of survival. My mother never had a bank balance or a business card, but she ran a whole world inside four walls. With very little money and even less help, she raised three daughters, cooked every meal, managed every crisis, and carried every expectation without once asking for applause. I never saw her break. Her resilience wasn't loud. It was rhythmic, like breath; always there, always steady.

My father, on the other hand, was fire. He burned quickly, mainly when his pride or pain was triggered. Society was harsh to men who raised only daughters. The whispers came easily: "What will girls do? Who will carry the name forward?" When neighbours made such remarks, I saw a storm rise in him. That bitterness often reached us, not because we deserved it, but because he didn't know where else to direct the shame society had thrust upon him. But even through that fury, there was a man who never missed a bill, never forgot to buy us textbooks, and never stopped believing that we were worth the effort.

Growing up, I tried to understand them both, not just as parents but as people. My mother, who hushed her dreams so that ours could subsist, and my father, whose anger came from a place of inoperable pride and deep responsibility. Between them, I learned two lessons that shaped me: silence can carry strength, and anger can sometimes mask pain.

We three sisters were different notes of the same song. I was the eldest, the one who observed more than I spoke. I didn't always have answers, but I knew I had to stay steady. When our family split temporarily due to tensions with our grandparents, I was only ten years old. But I remember trying to be the bridge. I would talk to my grandmother about my father with softness. I would sit next to Papa and say, "Dadi misses you." I didn't have the words for it then, but what I was saying was, "Let's not fall apart."

Our bond as sisters was formed not in luxury but in shared rooms, whispered fears, and midnight tears. The night before I left for Navodaya, we sat together in silence. None of us knew what to say. And then one of us started crying. Then all of us did. It was not just about me leaving. It was about change, about childhood coming to an end, about knowing that from now on, we would all carry a little more of it alone. I remember my youngest sister clutching my dupatta and whispering, "Don't forget us." I told her, "How could I? You're my heartbeat."

Being the eldest daughter in an Indian family comes with an unspoken set of responsibilities. You become the second mother, the fixer, the listener, the one who must not falter. The eldest daughter in a family is often not just a child but a quiet force expected to mature more quickly, relinquish responsibilities earlier, and understand more deeply than anyone else around her. She is raised, sometimes unconsciously, to be the backup parent, the emotional anchor, the one who must stay strong even when she is breaking inside. Long before she knows who she is, the world around her begins shaping her into who she must be. People say things like "You're the eldest; you should know better" or "Your siblings look up to you," and so she starts folding her needs away, like laundry, neatly and without protest. She watches her mother hold the house together, and without ever being asked, she begins to do the same. She gives her younger siblings the last piece of a sweet fruit, even when she is hungry, and learns to keep her worries quiet so her parents don't feel more pressure. She also becomes the first one to adjust and the last one to be asked how she is doing. She stays up to help with homework she has already outgrown; she sits quietly when plans change to favour someone else, and she hears thank you far less often than she hears requests. She does not complain because no one taught her how to, and she does not rebel because someone always needs her to hold it together.

In real life, she is the one who picks her sister up from tuition in the rain without an umbrella, who says she is not tired even after a full day of office work and kitchen chores, who gives up her dream job offer because her family needs her closer to home. She carries the guilt of not doing enough, even when she is doing everything. Yet somehow, her strength is not loud, and her love is not dramatic. It is in the quiet way she checks if everyone has eaten, the gentle way she irons her father's shirt for his big meeting and the smile she gives her mother after serving dinner, even when her plate is still empty.

The eldest daughter is made strong by the endless expectations, the unspoken rules, and the deep love that teaches her to care before she learns to breathe freely. Her story is not always told, but it is lived in millions of homes, in a million quiet sacrifices, and in a million women who learned to carry the world with both hands and still hold space for others to rest. I signed that contract without even knowing it. I handled things on my own, made choices carefully, and took responsibility for more than just my life. I was the insurance policy no one had asked for, but everyone quietly depended on me.

Even now, when I look back, I don't remember dramatic scenes of confrontation or rebellion. What I remember are small, ordinary moments that demanded extraordinary strength, my mother skipping meals to feed us during tight months, my father keeping his worries to himself and only exhaling when we slept, and the way my sisters and I built our world out of school projects, old storybooks, and bedtime laughter.

Our home didn't echo with declarations of love. But it pulsed with it. It was in the way Ma saved the softest roti for me. It was in the way Papa kept our old report cards like treasure. It was in the way my sisters celebrated my smallest wins as if they were their own. Love in our home was never a performance. It was a presence.

And now, as an adult, I realise how much of that strength I carry. When life demands more from me, I think of Ma holding everything together without ever asking for rest. When society questions my choices, I think of Papa facing the world with pride, even when the world tries to make him feel small. When I feel the weight of everything I have to be, I think of my sisters; our bond, our tears, our shared courage.

As a child, I would look at pictures of Indian temples in history books and old magazines with deep fascination, wondering how such magnificent structures were built at a time when there were no machines, no modern tools, and nothing to make human life easier, yet they rose with such grace and detail that they seemed almost unreal. I was in awe of how people, with their bare hands and unmatched dedication, could create something so beautiful, so intricate, and so lasting. When I grew older and visited a few temples myself, I was struck by how they had stood tall for centuries, weathering storms, time, and change, and still remained rooted in silence and strength. As I walked through their corridors and looked up at their grand ceilings, I began to understand that what truly held these temples together were not just their outer carvings or rituals but their pillars, strong, grounded, and quietly powerful. It was those pillars that carried the weight of centuries, and I realised at that moment that true strength often lies in what holds everything together without needing to be seen or celebrated.

This chapter of my life is not about achievement. It is about acknowledgement. It is about the quiet pillars that held me when I didn't even know I was falling. It is about loud love that never needs to be said out loud to be heard. It is about the continuity of strength, passed from Ma's worn hands to mine, and from mine to my sisters, and now, to the future we are all helping to build.

One must understand that no family is perfect. It is flawed, messy, and sometimes painful. But it is also the first place you learn what love can look like when it doesn't need validation. In our home, love didn't shout. But it stayed. And that, I now know, is the loudest kind of love there is.

Chapter 9: Those Who Held The Ladder

"No one climbs a mountain alone. Every step is a gift from those who held the rope steady."

Unknown

Success in life often appears to be a solitary climb up a ladder that we scale with determination, hard work, and perseverance. However, we occasionally forget that nobody climbs alone. Every climb has a person behind it who keeps the ladder steady, ensures we don't fall when we tremble, encourages us to keep going when we stop, and has faith in us when we start to doubt ourselves. The climb wouldn't be possible without these silent supporters, who might not always be seen at the summit. I learned that progress isn't always linear while playing Snakes and Ladders as a child. Sometimes, you slide back, and other times, you get up fast. However, the ladder was always a symbol of hope; a quick boost to your destination. Later in life, I noticed ladders everywhere: the ones we used to adorn our doorways with lights and flowers during festivals, transforming ordinary entrances into festive spaces; the stairways in colleges and schools that helped me become more knowledgeable and self-assured; and the tall buildings I entered with anxiety as a young adult pursuing dream. All of these ladders, both real and metaphorical, represented change, aspiration, and elevation. A human presence was also present behind everyone: a teacher opening doors to learning, a parent getting up early so I could study, a friend encouraging me when I faltered, and a partner illuminating the path ahead.

The silent strength of my parents, teachers, sisters, friends, and colleagues, who supported me through every stage of life, is what I owe to every step of my journey. Even when I stumbled, their support remained unwavering, their belief remained strong, and their words of encouragement were frequently silent. They guided my path as I reached upward rather than walking in front of or behind me. They formed the very organisation that made the climb possible, so they weren't just a part of it.

A father's love is not always spoken, but it is felt in a thousand quiet ways. He is the steady rhythm beneath the chaos, the calm in the background that makes everything else possible. He teaches without speaking much, showing us, what strength looks like when it is humble and what love feels like when it is constant. His days are long, and his worries are often unshared, yet he shows up again and again without expecting anything in return. We learn from him how to carry weight without complaint, how to keep going when it's hard, and how to protect what matters most. He does not ask to be noticed, but his presence becomes the reason we feel safe. He is the one who fixes things without being asked, who remembers what we forget, and who quietly holds the world together when it feels like it's falling apart. A father is not just a provider. He is a quiet guardian of dreams, a builder of courage, and the first man who teaches us that real strength is gentle. In his silence, we find comfort. In his footsteps, we find direction. And in his love, which is steady, selfless, and enduring, we find home.

From the very beginning, my parents have been the core of my existence. They are indispensable, instrumental, and irreplaceable in every sense. If life is a journey of climbing, they were the ones who steadied the base when I had nothing to stand on. My father appeared strict and short-tempered on the outside, but he was a deeply caring and responsible man. With a modest salary of just ₹10,000, he raised three daughters, supported five sisters, and cared for ageing parents. He had no savings until we completed our education because every rupee he earned went into building our future. Despite the pressure, he never took a single loan; for him, every expense had to be covered by honest earnings, not borrowed money. His temper was shaped by stress, not by a lack of love. His responsibilities were many, but he carried them alone without complaint. He never spoke of sacrifice, yet every moment of his life was devoted to fulfilling the needs of others. He gave silently, consistently, and selflessly. We couldn't afford store-bought notebooks, so we bought white or ruled pages in bulk and stitched them into simple notebooks at home. These humble bundles became our treasures. Even our Nataraj pencil boxes were treated with great care as if they were tools from an engineer's kit: reliable, lasting, and not to be misplaced. My father never bought anything for himself. Even during festivals or family weddings, he wore his old clothes with quiet dignity. Yet for us, he always ensured there were new outfits, lovingly chosen and neatly packed.

My mother, ever watchful and tender, always ate her meal last. She waited until everyone else had been served and was satisfied before sitting down quietly with her plate. It was not asked of her, but it was how she loved: with patience, with humility, and with presence. There was never any complaint, only a deep sense of purpose. Even my grandparents, especially my grandfather, who passed away when I was in the eleventh standard, always blessed us with silent prayers and gentle hopes. But it was my parents who were the pillars of our lives. Every step I have taken, every dream I have dared to chase, has been made possible by their quiet sacrifices and relentless belief in me. Their love built a home. Their discipline gave it shape. And their sacrifices gave it a soul.

My parents lived a life of restraint and sacrifice, not because they had no dreams of their own, but because they poured everything, they had into building ours. Their endurance was not dramatic or loud but steady, firm, and constant. When financial storms arrived, my mother would part with her jewellery, one bangle at a time, to keep the house running without ever letting us feel the burden. Their priority was always our education. Despite their modest means, they found and arranged the best tuition teacher for the three of us, believing that knowledge was the most significant inheritance they could offer.

My sisters were not just part of my childhood; they were the heart of it. We didn't just grow up together; we grew into each other. From the cracked pages of shared textbooks to the whispered dreams exchanged under a mosquito net, everything was built on togetherness. When life felt uncertain, their belief in me was unwavering. When I felt invisible to the world, they saw me completely. They celebrated my most minor victories as if they were their own and stood beside me in every heartbreak, quietly holding space when I had no words. Their love was fierce, gentle, and constant, a kind of bond that neither time nor distance could ever touch. I have carried their laughter in my silence, their strength in my doubt, and their prayers in my every leap. Being their sister has been my life's most enduring privilege and my quiet, lifelong source of courage.

In life, when the time comes to step away from home and we are far from the arms that once held us, it is the teacher who becomes our new shelter. My schooling began in a village where blackboards were worn, and classrooms echoed with simplicity. We carried seating mats in our school bags, unrolling them each day to sit and learn. That mat was our desk, our seat, and sometimes even our shelter from the dust. It was in this humble setting that the foundation of my learning was laid.

At school, when the world widened beyond home, my teachers became gentle guides, steady as my parents. They became my voice when I doubted myself, and my mirror when I forgot who I was. They woke before us, stayed after us, and gave without ever keeping score. Their love was quiet. Their sacrifice was unseen. But their impact was eternal. They were time-givers, silence-breakers, and soul-shapers. I still remember the day my Physics teacher handed me the lab keys. It was not just an object but a gesture that said, I trust you. And sometimes, that is all a student needs; one person to believe in her.

In that silent lab, between circuits and shadows, I began to see the outline of the person I could become. Every subject we studied felt alive because it was presented to us with genuine passion and enthusiasm. Biology unfolded as the story of life itself, from the birth of the first cell to the emergence of Earth's most extensive and intricate species. It revealed how the universe came alive, one organism at a time. Chemistry showed me how two completely different elements can come together to create something entirely new, through bonds, reactions, and transformations. It taught me that even opposites, when combined with the right intent and balance, can form powerful, lasting connections. Maths taught me that even the most difficult questions have answers if we look deep enough. Social Science helped me understand people, and Literature taught me how to embrace their stories.

The co-curriculars were not just extras. They were essential. In music, I found the echo of my voice. In the arts, I found expression when words would fail me. In sports, I discovered that falling is not failing as long as you rise again. Then came a turning point in my life. Navodaya was much more than just a school. It felt like a sacred place where I was not only educated but truly shaped. I learned patience, honesty, and how to believe in myself.

My teachers helped me understand how to think critically, ask questions, and grow with confidence. Navodaya gave me sunlight, just as my parents gave me the soil. With blessings in their hearts and books in their hands, my teachers stood in that nourishing light. I often think of them as living embodiments of Maa Saraswati and Lord Ganesha. These are not just decorations. They represent knowledge, rhythm, and introspection. From my teachers, I received love without conditions, guidance without pressure, and wisdom shared in quiet grace. Even now, wherever life takes me, I carry those lessons with me. I would not have reached this point on my own. The people who guided me back then are still with me, supporting me with love.

College at VSSUT continued that journey. I found new mentors, friends who became family, and a growing belief in my abilities. At Made Easy, the coaching institute, I learned the rigour and clarity necessary to excel in competitive exams. At IIT Kanpur, I was challenged both academically and personally, expanding not only my knowledge but also my worldview. Each teacher in these institutions gave me more than just instruction; they provided mirrors in which I saw my strengths and areas for improvement. I learned that proper education is not about answers; it is about learning how to ask better questions.

Likewise, at every step, friends walked beside me. They offered laughter when the days were heavy, silence when words failed, and shoulders when tears flowed. My sisters carried hope in their eyes for me. Their pride in my journey gave me strength, and their unwavering belief reminded me of what I was capable of. They were not just family but lifelines.

Today, when I sit quietly and look back, I realise that every step I took was held by someone else's hand. Many of those hands were dusty with chalk, worn from correcting notebooks, and tired from standing too long, but they never let go. I miss them. I miss their presence, quiet encouragement, and the strength they provided without ever seeking recognition. In a world that measures success in money and medals, they were the rare ones who asked only one thing. Are you okay?

It was also at Navodaya where I met him, a classmate, a silent admirer, and eventually, the man who would become the most crucial part of my life. I was focused on my studies and my goal to become a helping hand for my father. I did not allow myself to be distracted, so I kept my distance. I had no idea then how deeply he would be woven into the story of my life.

Years passed, and life brought us back into each other's orbit. A casual phone call, sparked by curiosity, led me to discover that he was preparing for the IIT-JEE entrance exam. I wished him well and stepped away, thinking that was the end. But destiny had written a different script. Then, through a common friend, a contact was established again during my second year of engineering. That's when I found out he had been accepted into IIT Delhi to study Civil Engineering. We began talking again, cautiously, as if we both sensed something meaningful was unfolding. One day, he sent a message that changed everything. He said he could not be just a friend. He wanted something real or nothing at all. That was the moment I knew I was ready. I said yes.

From that point on, we walked together and supported each other through every phase of life. Internships, coaching classes, placements, long-distance calls, and early struggles came one after the other, but we stood side by side through it all. Whether we lived in different cities or faced demanding schedules, we found strength in small gestures and quiet understanding. He helped me settle into new places, taught me how to ride a bicycle so I could move around campus, and made sure I never felt alone. I encouraged him as he prepared for his MBA and watched him work toward his goals with determination. There were moments when we hardly met, yet the connection never faded. When I was tired or overwhelmed, he was there with a calm, supportive presence. He made difficult days easier and joyful moments brighter. Even when things were not easy with his family, he chose me with clarity and commitment. Over time, we built a bond that could weather pressure, distance, and change. A true life partner is someone who offers strength without asking, who remains steady when everything else feels uncertain, and who celebrates your wins as if they were his own. In him, I found a friend, a companion, and a quiet source of courage. He has been with me in silence and celebration, and that is what love truly means.

At work, I found myself surrounded by guides once again; senior officers who not only showed me the ropes but also shaped the way I approached my role. They helped me read the unspoken language of the office, the little things that made the culture what it was, and they mentored me through every task with patience and precision. From them, I learned the steady pace of research, the give-and-take of teamwork, and the quiet discipline it takes to see a project through. They showed me how to stay calm when the pressure built, how to carry responsibility without letting it crush me, and how to stand tall in rooms where every decision mattered.

And then came the most profound teacher of all: life. It did not arrive with a timetable or a lesson plan. Its teachings came through delays, setbacks, heartbreaks, and failures. There were no warnings, no notes to prepare from, yet its lessons lasted far longer than anything found in textbooks. Life taught me that even when

I fall, I can rise stronger. That loss, though painful, creates space for clarity. Patience is not a weakness, but a quiet power. Through struggle and hope, life became the teacher I could never outrun and never outgrow. It showed me that actual growth often hides in the most ordinary days and that the most challenging moments are usually the most honest chapters in our story.

In the moments when I felt I had nothing left, I sensed God beside me. He never arrived with a sign or a grand display. He was quiet, constant, and steady. I did not always see Him, but I felt Him; in a stranger's kind word, a phone call at just the right time, or an inner strength that appeared when I thought I had none. In confusion, He brought calm. In loneliness, He sent comfort, sometimes through silence, sometimes through something as simple as a breeze. He never pushed. He stayed. When I cried without speaking, I believed He understood. Over time, I came to know that faith is not built on miracles or spectacles. It is built on the quiet certainty that you are never truly alone.

As I reflect on my journey, I am most moved by the people who stood beside me when I needed them the most. Some offered strength when I had none. Others believed in me when I had stopped believing in myself. Their support was not loud or fleeting. It lived in stillness, in presence, and in the small acts that never made headlines but changed everything. They were the ground beneath my steps, the force behind every bit of progress, and the reason I kept moving forward. Their kindness became my foundation. Because I was lifted with such care and love, I now carry a quiet responsibility to do the same for others. Growth is not only about rising higher; it's also about reaching new heights. It is also about reaching back, offering a hand, and helping someone else rise with you. That, to me, is the true mark of becoming.

PART IV: SERVICE AND SELF DISCOVERY

Chapter 10: Antarctica Called My Name

"Antarctica was also a male bastion; women scientists weren't allowed there before 1956."

Professor Sudipta Sengupta, one of the first women to conduct field research on the continent

Lying almost entirely under an archaic, shimmering mantle of ice, Antarctica remains the coldest and most isolated continent on Earth. It is a place of extremes, with winter temperatures falling below eighty degrees Celsius, summers bringing endless sunlight, and winters shrouded in total darkness. Straddled by the turbulent Southern Ocean, Antarctica is largely untouched by politics, protected for science and peace under the Antarctic Treaty signed by various nations. This part of the world is both a geographic wonder and, in the words of British broadcaster and biologist David Attenborough, 'a barometer of the health of our planet.' The region holds Earth's climate history beneath its towering glaciers and undiscovered ice shelves, which serve as records over millennia. Scientists endure bone-shattering storms to study the shifting patterns of sea ice, melting glaciers, and the tenacity of life in one of the harshest environments known to exist today. Those findings shape our understanding of humanity's future with terrifying clarity. Visiting this continent reveals the worrying vulnerability our world truly has, while the harm that needs to come to protect this remaining marvel is all too apparent.

With each step of my journey, I have come to believe that the adage "Fortune favours the brave" is true. Andhari, a small village tucked into the heart of Odisha's Jajpur district, is where my story began. Life there moved slowly, bathed in silence and simplicity.

Mornings began with the rustling of palm leaves and the songs of birds echoing across the paddy fields. The scent of Earth, woodsmoke, and sun-warmed grain lingered in the air. You could hear the rhythmic creak of hand pumps, the splash of water in metal pots, and the soft laughter of women drawing water under the early light. Afternoons hummed with stillness. Evenings fell without drama. They settled in like an old friend, quiet and unhurried, wrapping the village in shadows and calm.

Our home was modest. My father worked as a pharmacist at the local primary health centre in Jakhapura. He was a man of few words and steady purpose. My mother was a homemaker whose patience and devotion held our family together like an invisible thread. As the eldest daughter, I grew into responsibility early. But I carried dreams too. Dreams that reached beyond our lanes of pressed mud, beyond the lantern-lit corners of our home. I studied through summer blackouts, poring over books under the dim glow of kerosene lamps. I walked to school during the rain, wading through puddles and narrow footpaths. And yet, with every storm and every step, my conviction only deepened. I believed that no matter how far I came from, no wall could keep out a determined heart.

Life in the village was as beautiful as it was difficult. Electricity came and went like a passing wind. In the peak of summer, the nights would grow unbearably warm and still, only to be made worse by sudden power cuts. During the monsoon, thunder split the skies, and lightning often struck the village transformer. Sometimes we had to wait for days before repairs arrived. In those moments, light came not from switches, but from preparation. Every household kept multiple lanterns. There was one for cooking, another for studying, and a few more just in case. Kerosene was stored like treasure. When shop-bought lanterns broke or ran out, we made our own from used tins. Their small flames danced against the walls, stubborn and defiant, just like us. Despite these conditions, the village thrived in its way. Each home had its pond where fish glided beneath lotus leaves. Small gardens overflowed with coriander, pumpkins, brinjal, and spinach. We drank milk from our cows, collected eggs from hens that wandered freely, and cooked food that tasted of soil and sun. No one ate alone when something special was made. A warm, sweet bowl of Kheer always made its way to a neighbour's doorstep, wrapped in nothing but care. We did not need to ask. It was understood. We did not depend on shops or markets. In every village, the hum of sewing machines echoed through courtyards. Mothers, daughters, and grandmothers stitched and altered, not just clothes, but memories. A torn hem was never thrown away; it found new life in the hands of the careful. What we lacked, we mended. There was no waste, only care and renewal. Life was honest, rooted, and slow. And from that soil, I rose.

In 2015, I joined a Space Research company in Ahmedabad. That moment was a turning point. I began working on Earth Imaging Satellites, contributing to missions that helped monitor our coastlines, assess damage during floods, and support farmers with land use data. As time passed, my responsibilities grew. I became part of India's deep space missions beyond Earth and the moon. The work demanded technical precision and clear thinking. But it also required vision; the kind I had first imagined by the light of a lantern. These projects taught me how deeply science is woven into the fabric of everyday life. They shaped my belief that science is not just discovery. It is a service.

In addition to my technical work, I began volunteering at science exhibitions and outreach programs. I visited schools and colleges to share stories of satellites, missions, and the power of human curiosity. One of the most unforgettable experiences was representing my company at an Inspire Camp for students from Ladakh. It was November, and the cold was intense. Water pipes were frozen, and mobile networks barely worked. Despite these challenges, students from different corners of Ladakh crossed rugged mountain passes to attend.

I spoke to them about space, about the stars, and about the endless possibilities that science and technology can unlock. Their eyes were wide with curiosity, and their questions came quickly, one after another. In their excitement, I saw my own younger self. That interaction was very special to me. It reminded me that these sessions are not just lectures. They are moments of connection. They are quiet beginnings, where each child walks away carrying a small spark of hope. One day, that spark may grow into something much bigger.

When I was selected for the 37th Indian Scientific Expedition to Antarctica, I knew my life was about to undergo a significant change. I became the first woman from Odisha to represent India on the icy continent, joining a group so small it felt almost secret. Till now, fewer than thirty Indian women had ever made that journey before me. Scientists, doctors, and engineers each had walked those frozen shores carrying the weight of their own stories. Now it was my turn. The thought settled on me like the silence of snow. This was more than an opportunity. It was a reckoning of everything that had brought me here. Every early morning in Andhari, every exam, every choice, every quiet act of endurance. I carried them all with me like tools, like armour.

The realisation of my selection came slowly, like light creeping into a dark room. It was not loud or triumphant. It was quiet, steady, and full of life. I felt pride, yes, but it was laced with something more profound: a sense of sacred duty, of being entrusted with something rare and precious. I thought of that girl in the village, sitting cross-legged with a book and a kerosene lamp. I thought of all the moments when giving up would have been easier. Now, standing on the edge of something so vast, I felt nothing but stillness. It was as if the pieces of my past had assembled themselves into a staircase, and I was now at the final step before the sky opened.

The entire team was electric with anticipation. On the day our selection was officially announced, we looked at one another and felt the shift. We had crossed into a new chapter. Our first stop was Auli, a mountain town in Uttarakhand, where our physical training would begin. Though I had seen snow before, being surrounded by mountains blanketed in white was something else entirely. The cold did not ask for permission. It pierced through clothing and clung to your bones. The air was thin and sharp. Our breaths became clouds, our fingers stiff before drills even began.

"This place is not for the faint-hearted," one of the ITBP instructors told us on a frost-bitten morning. "You will either come back with your head held high, or not at all." His words were not dramatic. They were honest. Every training session confirmed that. We learned to tie rescue knots with numb fingers. We scaled icy ridges, clinging to ropes that cut into our gloves. We descended cliff faces, learning to trust our equipment and, more importantly, our bodies. We rehearsed emergencies until muscle memory replaced panic. Our limbs ached. Our backs burned. But every drop of sweat was a badge we wore without complaint.

One evening, as I sipped hot tea while my boots steamed from the snow, a fellow trainee said to me, "You never stop pushing. It's like you're carrying something more than just your backpack." I smiled quietly. He was right. I carried the dreams of a village, the hopes of a family, and the silent strength of every woman who had paved the way in silence.

Before we began our mountain training, we were sent to AIIMS in New Delhi for a complete medical evaluation. It was the first gatekeeper, and it was thorough. Everything was thoroughly tested, including physical health, dental records, psychological stability, vision, reflexes, cardiac endurance, and more. The hallways were full of applicants waiting for their turn. Some read quietly. Others sat in silence. I sat among them, not nervous but resolute. I had not come this far to turn back. If a hurdle arose, I would leap. If I had to wait, I would wait with patience. But I would not walk away. I owed that to the girl who once memorised formulas by lantern light, and to every challenge I had already overcome.

After the icy silence of Auli, we moved to Goa for fire training. It felt like entering another world. The air was thick with salt and humidity. Coconut trees swayed against the sun, and the sound of waves added an almost musical rhythm to our schedule. But we were not there for rest. Goa demanded a different kind of readiness. Our drills began before the sun had finished rising. We practised emergency responses, learning to extinguish fires, evacuate from smoke-filled rooms, and operate rescue equipment with speed and precision. One of the most challenging drills required us to crawl through a tunnel filled with artificial smoke. The visibility was almost zero. I moved slowly, knees against metal, heart pounding as the smoke pressed into my mask. Every breath was a decision. Every motion required trust. I couldn't see where I was going, but I kept telling myself, 'You are meant for this, keep going.'

In the evenings, when training paused and the light turned golden, Goa revealed its warmth to us. We walked back to our quarters in uniforms streaked with ash and sweat, but something about the sea air softened the edges of our exhaustion. I would look up at the deepening sky and feel a quiet peace settle over my thoughts. Every challenge I faced, every drop of effort I gave, was building someone new. I was not preparing for a trip. I was preparing for transformation.

The morning of our departure arrived like a dream wrapped in silence. It was not chaotic. It was calm, measured, and heavy with meaning. I stood at the threshold of something that felt both deeply personal and profoundly historical. My bags were packed with layers of thermal gear, scientific instruments, and carefully folded letters from home. But they also carried something less visible; the weight of quiet preparation, the echo of small sacrifices, and the long, slow breath of a journey finally exhaling.

The morning of our departure was calm, almost too quiet for a day I had waited for so long. My bags were packed with care, from the thickest thermal jackets to the smallest keepsakes tucked between layers of clothing. Each item felt like a piece of my journey, carrying with it the memory of late nights, early mornings, and the voices that had encouraged me along the way. I stood for a moment before leaving, letting the stillness sink in, and felt a quiet strength rise within me. This was not just another trip. It was the moment everything I had worked for began to take shape.

We flew first to New Delhi, then to Johannesburg, and finally landed in Cape Town. With each stop, the air changed. The light shifted. The scenery grew sharper, more distant, more elemental. Cape Town felt like a line drawn between two worlds; one I had known, and one I was only beginning to understand. The mountains stood tall in the distance. The ocean stretched endlessly, and the air carried the kind of silence that asked you to listen.

Our team was divided in Cape Town. Those assigned to inland stations boarded aircraft bound for Antarctica's inner terrain. I was among those assigned to study sea ice and glaciers. We would travel by ship. The vessel, a Russian icebreaker named *Ivan Papanin*, towered above the docks like a floating citadel. Built for polar missions, it was part science station, part survival fortress. It had seven decks. The rooms, constructed from steel containers, were equipped with compact furniture and attached restrooms. There was a small gym, a mess hall, and a narrow corridor that always smelled faintly of diesel and sea salt.

The crew was entirely Russian. The captain spoke little English but carried an authority that needed no translation. The vice-captain was an Indian scientist of few words and much respect. On board were twenty-five researchers from across India and beyond; specialists in biology, glaciology, meteorology, and geomagnetism. Despite our different languages and backgrounds, we shared one destination. One purpose.

I wasn't alone on the expedition. Alongside me was a senior scientist from our office, a man with more than twenty years of experience in climate research, whose knowledge of the field ran as deep as the landscapes we were about to explore. Our task was to study the movement of glaciers and the changing behaviour of sea ice in response to global warming. We spent the first few days adjusting to the ship's layout, familiarising ourselves with emergency protocols, setting up our instruments, and falling into the rhythm of a journey where the ocean was always in motion.

And then we entered the Southern Ocean. It was relentless. As the ship pushed through the Furious Fifties and into the Screaming Sixties, we entered a realm unlike any I had ever known. These latitudes are infamous for their powerful westerly winds, uninterrupted by land. The result is a sea that moves with force and fury. The waves rose like dark walls, curling and breaking with a rhythm that could not be predicted. The ship rocked from side to side, pitched forward and back, creaking and groaning like a living thing.

It was a world of motion and disorientation. Sea sickness spread like wildfire. Nearly eighty per cent of those onboard, including seasoned crew members and even the ship's chef, fell ill. The air inside was heavy with silence, nausea, and the thick scent of fuel. Trays remained untouched. Doors stayed closed. The corridors fell quiet. Strangely, my body did not give in. I was one of the few who could stand, move, and focus. In that moment, I found clarity.

With the help of one or two others, I began preparing simple meals, such as khichdi and tomato chutney; comfort food that could soothe unsettled stomachs. We moved through the cabins, bowl in hand, checking on each person and offering warmth where it was needed. The ship no longer felt like a scientific mission. It felt like a floating family, bruised but bound by quiet care. My hands stayed steady. My thoughts stayed sharp. I was not focused on the waves outside. I was focused on the kindness we could extend to one another.

Eventually, the waters began to settle. The sky lightened. The wind eased, and Antarctica appeared. We carried out our research with focus and respect. We walked across fields of ice that stretched endlessly into the blue. We recorded data, tracked glacial drift, and monitored sea ice. The cold was unforgiving. The silence was complete. And we worked as though time itself was watching.

Then, just as our expedition neared its end, the ocean reminded us again that nothing here could be predicted.

We had survived the sea, the cold, the storm, and the unknown. And in doing so, we had discovered not just the continent, but something much quieter and more profound: the endurance that lives in all of us, waiting for a reason to rise.

As we approached the coast of Antarctica, the world began to transform around us in ways I had never imagined. It was as if nature itself was preparing to reveal something sacred. The sky took on a pale blue that seemed to stretch forever, not the blue of tropical skies or mountain peaks, but a lighter, colder hue, as though the light itself had been filtered through ice. The ocean, which had churned and raged just days before, now softened into a silvery calm. The waves flattened, the wind fell to a whisper, and a quiet settled over everything. It felt as though the world was holding its breath.

Icebergs appeared in the distance, each one gliding with silent majesty. Some looked like castles with sharp towers and glinting edges. Others resembled sleeping animals or temples carved by time. Their stillness was striking. There was no sound as they passed, only presence. I stood on the deck, wrapped tightly in my parka, my breath forming small clouds in the air, and whispered to myself, 'This is the edge of the Earth.' A fellow researcher beside me chuckled gently. "You look like you just saw a miracle," he said. I turned to him and smiled. "I think I did."

The coastline emerged slowly; first, a pale streak on the horizon, and then, white cliffs, wide shelves of snow, and glacial mountains appeared, shimmering beneath the sun. There were no trees. No buildings. No signs of life, except for a single bird circling high above. And yet, it felt more alive than anywhere I had ever been.

We landed with quiet resolve. Instruments in hand, we stepped onto the frozen continent. The snow crunched beneath our boots. The wind sliced through layers of clothing. The air smelled of salt and silence. We began our work by measuring the temperature of sea ice, tracking the rhythms of glacial melt, recording wind patterns, and measuring solar radiation. Each reading felt like a conversation with the Earth, each data point a whisper from the past.

The cold reached through every layer of protection. Our hands stayed wrapped in gloves, our faces covered. However, despite the discomfort, we continued. We worked without complaint, without pause. This was not a place for ease. It was a place for a purpose.

Communication was sparse. Satellite signals came and went. There were no daily calls, no distractions. In the evenings, we shared stories over bowls of soup. Some nights we listened to the wind. The research station felt like an island at the edge of the known world.

At night, I would step outside and look up at the southern sky. It was wide and clear, filled with stars that shone brightly against the silence of the Antarctic landscape. On some nights, I could see the auroras. They appeared like waves of colour gently moving across the sky, glowing in shades of green, pink, and violet. It felt like they were dancing, slow and graceful, in the stillness of the night.

In those quiet moments, I often thought of my parents. I remembered the lantern-lit evenings in Andhari, and the journey that had brought me from that small village to this distant and incredible part of the world. The sky above me seemed vast and familiar, holding all the places and people I had come from, and reminding me how far I had travelled.

There was peace in that silence. A peace unlike any I had known. It came not from comfort, but from clarity. In this place, there were no illusions. No pretence. Only truth. It taught me that the world still holds places that are untouched, unspoiled, and quietly majestic. And it reminded me of something else: that it is in the harshest places that we sometimes find the softest parts of ourselves.

When the time came to leave, I did not cry. I did not speak. I stood in the wind and let the cold settle on my face. I knew that this place would stay with me. Not just in memory, but in the way I saw the world. I had come to Antarctica for science. I returned with a deeper understanding of resilience, humility, and the vast, quiet courage that lies inside us all.

Chapter 11: Beyond Zero, Below Fear

"If your heart is in the right place, and your purpose is pure, even the ice will make way for you."

Dr. M.S. Swaminathan, Indian geneticist and plant breeder, administrator and humanitarian

Before we stepped onto the ice, we studied it from a distance. Sea-ice research is a field that demands not only precision but patience. Unlike land-based glaciers, sea ice forms, shifts, and vanishes in seasonal cycles, behaving more like a living skin stretched over the ocean than a fixed body of ice. Its sensitivity to changes in wind, temperature, and current makes it one of the most reliable indicators of climate instability. As part of the Indian scientific expedition, my role, along with a colleague, a senior scientist from my company, was to track these shifts, monitor the movement of glaciers, and collect data that could help map the real-time impacts of global warming in one of Earth's most remote and revealing locations.

Our journey began in Cape Town, where we boarded a Russian icebreaker designed for polar missions. The ship, a seven-deck vessel constructed with fortified steel, served as both a mobile laboratory and our temporary home. Every space inside was designed for utility rather than comfort. The rooms were compact, built from metal containers, and featured essential amenities, including heating and attached washrooms. The ship had a modest gym, a dining area, and a TV room that provided a quiet, shared space for the international group on board. The crew was entirely Russian, led by a commanding captain whose authority was apparent in every movement. Supporting him was a senior Indian scientist from the Ministry of Earth Sciences, who served as both a scientific lead and a cultural bridge for the Indian members of the team. I was the only Indian woman on the ship, but that distinction quickly gave way to the equalising demands of our mission. Each of us was measured not by our background but by our focus, effort, and ability to adapt.

In the early part of the voyage, the sea was calm. We moved steadily past floating icebergs that rose like sculptures from the water, their surfaces shaped by centuries of wind and salt. Beneath the surface of that calm, however, lay the unpredictable temperament of the Southern Ocean. As we crossed into the region known as the Furious Fifties, those latitudes between 50 and 60 degrees south, the ocean transformed. Winds picked up with relentless force, and waves began to crash against the ship with a wild rhythm. The vessel rolled and pitched without pause, making each step a challenge. Motion sickness spread quickly. Within days, nearly ninety per cent of the team had fallen ill, including the ship's cook. The mess hall grew quiet, and trays of uneaten food marked the days. It was a strange kind of stillness, one born from constant movement.

Through some stroke of luck, I remained well. While others rested and recovered, I took on simple tasks to lend a hand where I could. One day, I made khichdi and mashed tomato for everyone, a humble meal but warm and easy on the stomach. In those moments, even the smallest comforts became anchors of stability. We continued our work between the swells, recording ice formation patterns, collecting temperature data, and staying attentive to the changes around us. As the ship approached the Antarctic coastline, its speed was reduced. The waters began to harden, and instead of gliding, the hull had to press forward through resistance. The sound of ice breaking beneath us was steady and deep, like a warning whispered through metal. We were arriving not just at a geographic destination but at a threshold where nature sets its terms, and human presence is only temporary.

The first step on Antarctic land felt like stepping into another lifetime. After weeks spent swaying with the sea, the return to stillness was strangely disorienting. The body, once trained to anticipate the ship's constant motion, now braced for a movement that never came. As my boots pressed into the snow's shallow crust, they sank just enough to remind me that this ground, though solid, was breathing ice. A gust of wind tore through the open stretch, slicing across my cheek with such force and dryness it felt like it carried salt, not snow. This air had no softness. It had no scent. It did not drift. It struck and moved on. I paused, letting the silence settle. There were no birds overhead, no branches swaying, and no sound beyond the diminishing hum of the helicopter as it pulled away into the sky. Everything ahead of me was pale and vast. There was only rock, snow, and a horizon where the clouds had learned to stand still.

Bharati Station stood out brightly against the white, endless landscape surrounding it. The red and silver panels shimmered in the soft sunlight, making it look almost too perfect for such a wild setting. But once you stepped inside, it was alive with activity. You could smell dal and cumin cooking in the kitchen, blending with the sound of boots squeaking on the floor and gloves rustling as they dried near the heaters. In the command room, the computers flickered steadily while the water boiled for tea in old iron kettles. Everything had its place, and everyone followed a routine. The staff moved with a calm purpose, adapting to the quiet, indifferent rhythm of the continent. Off in the distance, other international stations, Chinese, Russian, Norwegian, peeked above the horizon. It felt like we were all part of a quiet team, connected not by our spoken words or politics but by the harsh weather we experienced together.

The sun never left us. It floated in the sky like a forgotten clock hand, rotating its position without ever dipping below the line of snow. Shadows moved in long arcs across the ground, but night never came. In this season, time became internal. There were no cues to sleep, no dusk to separate days. We ate when the clock told us it was morning. We rested not because the light dimmed but because our bodies began to slow. It was initially strange, then oddly freeing. The absence of night gave everything a soft glow that refused to fade. It became a landscape without endings.

Our days fell into a rhythm. Each morning began with preparation. Thick gloves were layered over thermal liners. Faces were wrapped in fleece. Equipment was checked, packed, sealed, and secured. Then we stepped outside into a brightness that felt eternal. The cold here was not a backdrop; it was a defining feature. It was a defining feature. It was a presence. It pressed into every seam of clothing. It coiled around the camera lenses. It crawled into the space between eyelashes. Every movement was deliberate. Every breath was visible.

On one of these days, we were flown to a ridge some distance from the station for glacial observation. The landscape below had no tracks, no signs of having been seen before. Snow curled across the ground in waves that resembled dunes. The wind was quiet but constant, shaping the edges of the rock into smooth, unreadable forms. As we worked, one of the team members noticed something near a cluster of stones. A few small, speckled eggs, half-buried in the snow, lay still and exposed in a shallow dip. Without thinking, he stepped closer, his curiosity getting ahead of caution.

The silence was shattered in an instant.

A piercing cry rang out from the sky, high and sharp enough to cut through the thick layers of our hoods. It came so suddenly that we instinctively froze. When we looked up, they were already upon us, dark birds moving fast, their wings stretched wide, slicing through the air like sharpened blades. These were skuas, powerful seabirds that dominated the Antarctic skies with authority. Larger than gulls and far more aggressive, they are known for their intelligence, speed, and relentless territorial defence. In this frozen wilderness, they rule the nesting grounds without compromise.

The first swoop came swiftly; a warning carried on the wind. One bird dove toward the head of a teammate who had unknowingly stepped too close to a shallow nest hidden between the rocks. Another targeted my right shoulder; its eyes locked onto mine with startling precision. I ducked just in time, feeling the force of wings as they rushed past my face. The others followed, loud and direct, circling in a pattern that felt strategic rather than chaotic. This was not random behaviour. This was a coordinated defence from creatures that had evolved in the harshest conditions on Earth and survived by never giving an inch.

Panic set in, but it came layered with instinct. We ran, not in straight lines, but with a calculated urgency, slipping and skidding across the uneven snow. Running on ice is not a fluid motion. It is cautious, uncertain, and intensely physical. Each step had to be judged before it landed. Every movement was made while bracing for the one that might go wrong. The skuas chased us the entire way, their sharp cries echoing above, their wings slicing through the frozen light. I could feel them closing in, could hear their shrill, angry calls growing louder as they followed us across the ice.

We finally reached a slope near the helicopter's landing site, and only then did the pursuit begin to fade. The birds circled once more, watching from above, and then drifted back toward their nesting grounds. We collapsed into the snow, breathing hard, our cheeks stinging from cold and adrenaline. None of us spoke for a while. There was nothing to say. The land had reminded us, through its most unyielding guardians, that our presence here was not a right, only a fragile permission. The skuas had drawn that boundary with their wings, and we had crossed it.

For a long time, none of us said anything. We sat in the snow, faces flushed with cold and adrenaline, silently absorbing what had just happened. It was not just a scare. It was a reminder. Antarctica does not welcome. It allows. And only for as long as you understand your place. This land belonged to no one. It answered to no rules. It offered beauty without invitation and consequence without warning. That day, we had forgotten where we were. The birds reminded us.

On the return journey, our ship struck an iceberg that had become submerged. The impact was sudden and unmistakable. The hull shuddered. Footsteps raced overhead. Alarms were not sounded, but urgency filled the air. Water had begun to enter the lower decks. The crew acted fast. Pumps were activated to control the ingress, but it was soon clear that continuing toward Cape Town without repairs would be reckless. The decision was made. We would return to the Antarctic coast. We were instructed to pack only essentials: our passports, critical documents, warm clothing, and a few personal items. There was no space for sentiment or delay. We stepped back onto Antarctic soil, this time not as scientists but as evacuees. Emergency flights operate only during the short Antarctic summer, from November to February. We were fortunate. A special flight was arranged to evacuate us. As the aircraft ascended and the white expanse faded beneath the clouds, I looked out the window and felt something I couldn't name. It was not fear. It was not relief. It was a strange calm that came from having faced uncertainty and held steady.

Back at Bharati, we waited for the rescue flight that would first take us to Maitri and then to Cape Town. The Antarctic runway looked like something imagined in a dream, consisting only of snow, sky, and a single aircraft resting in the middle of nowhere. No buildings. No fences. Only the raw simplicity of survival. There was fear, yes, but more than that, there was clarity. I had never felt more aware of what truly mattered.

When we reached Cape Town, everything felt slower and softer. The smell of trees, the sound of city life, and even the colour of the air felt different. I walked through botanical gardens, touched stone at the Cape of Good Hope, bought fragile eggshells to do shell painting during leisure time, and watched the ocean roll endlessly into itself. I did not speak much. I did not need to.

I had seen a world where night does not come, where birds defend with fury, and silence can roar. I had witnessed a continent both beautiful and indifferent. I had feared for my life, but I had also found within that fear a new sense of steadiness. What began as a fascination had become something more profound. It had become understanding. The kind that only cold, solitude and the unknown can carve into you.

The icy frontier of Antarctica did not ask for anything. It was only revealed. And in its vast, frozen mirror, I saw not just the planet but a part of myself I had never met before. I felt stronger.

This polar desert was never just a place on a map. It was a reckoning, a world of silence and storm that revealed more than it concealed. In that vastness, I encountered fear in its purest form, fascination that held me still, and adaptation that reshaped my very nature. I arrived as a scientist with instruments and objectives, but I returned as a woman transformed, steadier, quieter, and infinitely more aware. The continent stripped away comfort, routine, and assumption, leaving only the raw edge of endurance and the quiet strength born from surrender. No image, no data, no diary could fully capture what that frozen land gave me. Its winds carved something permanent into my spirit. Its light, which never dimmed, became part of how I now see the world. Antarctica, the white continent, did not welcome or embrace. It tested, revealed, and ultimately awakened. And though I left its shore behind, I carry its truth within me, like ice buried deep under layers of time, unchanged, unmoved, unforgettable.

Chapter 12: Discipline Below Zero

"India is not just a place on the map. It is a heartbeat, a rhythm, a set of values stitched into the skin."

Sardar Vallabhbhai Patel, Former Indian independence activist and Deputy Prime Minister of India

India is not just my country. It's part of who I am. When I greet someone with a namaste, it adds warmth to my voice. Taking off my shoes before entering a sacred space feels right to me. The familiar scent of mustard oil and turmeric evokes memories I cherish. Being Indian isn't just an identity I wear; it's a way of life. I feel proud when I'm abroad and find joy in sharing tea with strangers. It's the essence of who I am. And when I was sent to Antarctica, one of the most silent and lifeless corners of the Earth, it was this deep and unshakable Indianness that accompanied me.

In a land where flags meant little and borders were meaningless, I felt my national identity more strongly than ever before. The vastness of Antarctica made everything else feel small, except for the weight of where I came from. It gave me a sense of grounding and quiet dignity. The moment I entered Bharati Station, I felt it in my chest like a steady drumbeat. The cold outside had no mercy, but inside those red and silver walls, there was warmth, rhythm, and a deep sense of belonging. This was not just a structure but India, standing steady in a place where even shadows struggled to survive.

The deeper I went into the station, the more it reminded me of home. It was like stepping into a small but complete world, a floating island of familiarity surrounded by a sea of silence. The scent of jeera tempering in oil drifted out from the kitchen. A bell rang softly in the puja room during morning prayers. It was a quiet space within the Station, designed as a temple, where researchers from all religions could come to pray in their own way. Someone mopped the floor, humming an old Hindi tune without even realising it. Bharati had everything from a gym, a doctor's room, laundry facilities, and dining areas to storage rooms and carefully managed waste zones. Whether you were a scientist, a technician, or a carpenter, you washed your plates, folded your blanket, helped with odd repairs, and shared responsibilities without being asked. The ice outside could freeze steel, but inside Bharati, we kept each other warm with discipline, humour, and unspoken understanding.

Because of its unique geographical location, the sun did not set during the summer months. It was bright all day and all night, with sunlight pouring through even at midnight. There was no darkness to separate one day from the next. At first, it was disorienting to live without sunset or nightfall. We would wake up, eat, work, and sleep, all under the same unchanging light. Without the natural cues of morning or evening, we had to rely entirely on the clock to structure our lives. Time became something we followed by routine rather than by instinct. We created a schedule and stuck to it; eating meals at set hours, working according to task lists, and sleeping when the day's work was done. Slowly, that schedule gave us a sense of rhythm and balance. It became more than just a plan for the day. It became a way to stay focused and grounded, a quiet way of showing respect to the place we were in, to one another, and to the mission we were there to carry forward.

That mission was a human experience, a reminder that purpose can thrive even in the most desolate corners of the world. Our days were filled with surveys, data collection, equipment checks, and outdoor expeditions. We would be dropped near glaciers for observation, walking across untouched snow with instruments in hand and wonder in our eyes. Each field visit offered a different kind of silence, a different texture of light, and a different form of beauty that can never be fully described in words. Some days, we came back cold and exhausted. On other days, we returned with a sense of awe so deep that it made everything else feel irrelevant.

Long before we set foot on Antarctica, our journey began aboard the research ship, where we lived alongside the Russian crew. Space was limited, and routines were shared, but the one place that brought us together most often was the kitchen. There was only one galley on the ship, a compact space where Indian and Russian team members took turns, moved with unspoken coordination, and learned to respect each other's culinary rhythms. At first, there was hesitation: different spices, different ingredients, different styles of cooking. But curiosity has a way of dissolving boundaries. Some of us tasted Russian dishes for the first time; stews that warmed the bones, breads that felt dense and grounding. In return, whenever we prepared Indian meals, the aroma of jeera, cloves, and garam masala would rise into the air, curling through the narrow corridors like a silent invitation. Our Russian friends found our food fiery, their faces flushing at the first bite, eyes wide and glistening with unexpected heat. But they would laugh, nod in appreciation, and always come back for more. There was something deeply human about those shared meals; no language was needed, no formalities, just the comfort of food, the warmth of effort, and the joy of discovering each other through flavours that spoke of home.

Some moments felt almost magical. Once, during a brief break from fieldwork, we came across a group of seals stretched out like old kings on slabs of ice, their bellies rising and falling with calm indifference. Penguins passed us in perfect lines, their tiny feet shuffling across the snow as if on invisible roads. They stared at us without fear, and we stared back, unsure who was more curious. We clicked photos, not out of vanity but as proof that we had witnessed something rare and pure. These animals were not performers. They were not props. They were part of this continent's quiet dignity. We were only visitors.

Among the most meaningful moments we experienced at Bharati was the celebration of Republic Day. Surrounded by a vast frozen desert, with nothing but snow and sky in every direction, we came together to recreate the spirit of home. Preparations began days in advance. Decorations were carefully crafted by hand, banners were painted with patience, and a playlist of patriotic songs played softly in the background, filling the station with familiar energy. Everyone contributed in some way, whether through organising, decorating, cooking, or simply showing up with enthusiasm. Researchers from nearby international stations were also invited to join the celebration, and their presence added to the warmth and camaraderie of the day. When the Indian flag was hoisted outside, it rose against the icy wind and fluttered with a quiet strength that brought tears to many of us. It was a decisive moment. Scientists, engineers, technical staff, kitchen workers, and housekeeping teams all stood together, side by side. On that day, there were no titles or positions, only a shared sense of pride and belonging. Laddus were distributed after the flag ceremony, and that simple taste of home brought a deep understanding of comfort. There were no temples or churches, no festivals or city noise, no traffic or breaking news, but in that silent, snowy corner of the world, we felt more connected to India than ever before. Because your country is not just a place on a map, it is something you carry within you, kept alive through your memories, your actions, and the values you hold close.

While the celebrations continued, I closed my eyes for a moment and reminisced about my childhood days, when I used to watch the Republic Day parade on television every January 26th. Back home in India, Republic Day unfolded with grandeur and grace, especially in the heart of Delhi, where Rajpath transformed into a living symbol of the nation's strength and unity. The day began with the President's arrival, escorted by a mounted cavalry unit of the President's Bodyguard, in a procession steeped in tradition. The national flag was hoisted, the anthem echoed across the capital, and a 21-gun salute reverberated through the winter air. What followed was a parade unlike any other: regiments of the Army, Navy, and Air Force marched in perfect unison, tanks rolled past with thunderous pride, and fighter jets roared across the sky, leaving trails of saffron, white, and green. Schoolchildren danced in vibrant formations, tableaux from every state glided down the avenue, each telling a story of culture, struggle, or innovation. The energy was electric. Streets overflowed with spectators wrapped in woollens and waving flags, their eyes lit with pride. In that single morning, India showed the world it stood for diversity, discipline, and a democracy held together by dreams.

As Indian music composer A.R. Rahman's *"Vande Mataram"* played from loudspeakers across the neighbourhood, the morning would come alive with a quiet yet unmistakable energy. At school, we would dress in white salwar-kameez or neatly ironed shirts, with little tricolour badges pinned proudly to our chests. My sisters and I would tie our hair with ribbons in saffron, white, and green, and sometimes, we would paint tiny flags on our cheeks with sketch pens. In the neighbourhood, children would carry handmade flags and run around the colony as if they were leading a parade of their own. Women would wear crisp white saris or suits, accessorised with tricolour bangles and dupattas. Men would gather in white kurtas, often accompanied by a saffron or green stole draped across their shoulders. Someone would always put up flags outside balconies, tying them to bamboo sticks or curtain rods. The community park or school ground would be decorated with rows of tricolour streamers, and after the flag hoisting, trays of *laddoos, jalebis,* and chocolates would be passed around. People would greet each other with smiles and "Jai Hind," and even those who barely spoke during the year would stand side by side that morning. Republic Day would bring us all together, not with grandeur but with a shared pride in who we were and where we came from.

Service is not limited to uniforms, designations, or official duties. It comes in all shapes and sizes, and anyone, anywhere, can serve. Sometimes, it means standing at the front, leading with courage. At other times, it means quietly supporting from behind, ensuring that others have what they need to carry on. Service can be found in a soldier guarding the border, a doctor in a remote village, a teacher shaping young minds, or a neighbour offering food to someone in need. It can be as grand as risking your life or as humble as listening without judgment. What matters is not how visible the act is but the intention behind it. To serve is to care beyond yourself. It is to give, even when no one asks. It is to help, even when no one notices. Service is not a position. It is a way of thinking, a way of living, and a choice that anyone can make, at any moment, with whatever they have.

True service does not always look extraordinary. Most often, it is quiet and unfolds in the background. It resides in the small decisions people make, the thoughtful actions that may go unnoticed by the world but mean everything to those nearby. I came to understand this while living in Antarctica, truly. There were no award ceremonies, no applause, and no one keeping track of who did what. But each day, someone would rise early to heat water for those on the duty roster who were allowed to bathe. Bathing was not something we could do every day. Water was a limited resource, and every drop used had to be carefully treated afterwards. Nothing was wasted. Someone else would quietly vacuum the corridors before anyone else had stepped out of their rooms, making sure the living space stayed clean and comfortable. There were times when a person who had spent hours outside in the cold collecting data would still offer to help in the kitchen, to ease the burden on the cooking staff. These were not grand gestures. No one made announcements or expected thanks. They noticed what needed to be done and did it, not out of duty alone, but out of care for one another. That was the purest form of service.

I witnessed people discreetly sharing medicine with someone unwell. I noticed that colleagues often give up their meal portions without letting anyone know. When the wind outside was unbearable, and someone had to check the generator or fix a frozen pipe, they would go without hesitation. It wasn't about bravery but responsibility. We belonged to each other in that place, and that bond was not made of grand declarations. It was made with effort.

There were times when I was tired, afraid, or uncertain, but I always saw someone else step forward with calm, and that steadiness reminded me to do the same. Service is not always about what you do; it's also about how you do it. Sometimes, it is how you hold space for others. It is the patience in your voice, the discipline in your actions, and the willingness to do what is needed, even when it is not easy.

In Antarctica, I saw the best of human nature when no one was trying to prove anything. We lived in extreme conditions, but what carried us through was not equipment or protocol alone. It was about people choosing each other over comfort, duty over ease, and contribution over complaint.

When I returned to India, I carried this lesson with me quietly. I understood that service is not tied to place or position. It is something you carry in your values. Whether in a freezing station at the edge of the world or in the heart of your own home, it is the same. It's how you show up, how you give, and how you care.

Antarctica taught me many things about nature, science, and survival. But most of all, it taught me that the deepest form of service is not done for recognition. It is done out of love. For your team, for your country, and for the kind of person you hope to be when no one is watching.

That, to me, is discipline. And that is what I found; far below zero.

Discipline in India is not limited to uniform commands or formal instructions. It breathes through quiet moments of integrity and shared purpose. A soldier rising before dawn, a teacher preparing for class, a child tying the school tie just right, a doctor arriving early at a rural clinic; these are all quiet testaments to a value we hold close. Discipline is the thread that runs through our homes, institutions, and collective spirit. It does not need reminders. It simply continues as passed from hand to hand, voices that teach and hearts that serve.

In every part of India, from quiet villages to the heart of bustling cities, discipline is not only a value we speak about; it is a value we live by. It is a way of life that is passed down through generations. It lives in the quiet routines of families who rise early, work honestly, and serve without complaint. It shines through the eyes of a mother who folds her son's uniform with steady hands, knowing he is not going to a job but answering a call to serve the nation. She holds back her tears because she understands what it means to live with love and courage. Her sacrifice is not loud, but it is full of dignity.

India is a country shaped not only by its heroes in history books but by millions of unnamed citizens who choose integrity every day. It is built by teachers who mould young minds, by farmers who feed the nation with silent strength, by scientists who search for answers with discipline and hope, and by every honest hand that contributes to the whole. Service is not reserved for the few. It is a shared promise that runs through the hearts of many.

When I think of my country, I feel a sense of expansion in my chest. It is pride. It is gratitude and the knowledge that I belong to a land where sacrifice is made with love, duty is fulfilled with joy, and greatness is not declared but quietly lived. No wonder we say with such emotion and certainty, *Mera Bharat Mahaan.*

In Antarctica, surrounded by silence and snow, I saw those values echo in everything we did. There was no applause, only a shared understanding that each task mattered and each person mattered more. That spirit was not taught by climate or condition. It was brought from home, from India.

As we look ahead, we must carry this legacy with care and conviction. Our children are watching us. What we uphold in our lives becomes their foundation. When we choose responsibility over comfort, respect over indifference, and service over self-interest, we help India rise not through noise but through the quiet strength of good work done with sincerity.

Let this be our way of honouring the country we love. Not just in celebration but in daily conduct, in showing up, lifting others, and giving more than we take. Through this, India will not only shine but also lead. And we will know that we were part of that light; steady, strong, and true.

PART V: LEGACY AND LETTING GO

Chapter 13: Gravity Changed, She Did Not Fall

"When we are no longer able to change a situation, we are challenged to change ourselves."

Viktor E. Frankl, Austrian neurologist and psychologist

The year the world grew quiet was the year my life began to speak in a language I had never heard before. Outside, streets stood bare, shutters clanged shut, and the familiar hum of human movement faded into an uneasy stillness. Inside the Space Research company, the change was just as sudden. Laboratories that had once pulsed with purpose stood hushed, their machines waiting in dormancy, indicator lights blinking like patient lighthouses with no ships to guide.

For years, my days had been measured in launch countdowns, laboratory hours, and the weight of technical deadlines. I had learned to live by the pulse of precision, as if each day were a delicate dance between science and time. Now the rhythm faltered. Our work could not simply be carried home. The heart of our mission beats within specialised instruments that demand our physical presence. Without them, progress slowed to a crawl.

We adapted where we could. Documentation became our bridge to the future. Old projects were archived with care, their records like pressed flowers from another season. Meetings unfolded in masked clusters or flickered across screens. Ideas for future programmes were shaped like pencil sketches, waiting for the day they could be filled with colour. Attendance was staggered. We came to the office on alternate days, moving like figures in a slow-motion relay.

For most of my colleagues, this was a disruption. For me, it was something more. I was carrying my first child. Every trip to the office felt like walking a tightrope stretched between two worlds: the responsibilities of my role and the responsibilities of the new life within me. Every handshake avoided, every step through the lab, was weighed in a silent calculation of what mattered most: the mission at work or the mission in my womb.

Pregnancy is the quiet reordering of a universe. It shifts the axis on which you spin. Gravity changes. The body that had been entirely yours begins to work for two. Every decision becomes a negotiation between caution and courage. And during a pandemic, that shift feels even more pronounced. I was building life while the world outside was counting its losses in headlines and statistics.

When I first saw the confirmation, my emotions collided: a rush of surprise, a current of uncertainty, a whisper of excitement. My body felt the change before my mind could comprehend it. Nausea became my unwelcome companion, arriving without warning and leaving me drained. Fatigue clung to me like a heavy shawl. Still, I carried on with work, my secret tucked beneath layers of fabric and routine.

At my desk, as I examined complex data streams, I would occasionally rest my hand over my stomach, a small, unconscious gesture of protection. I found myself daydreaming about the baby in quiet moments, in the pause between reviewing technical data and answering emails, while walking down the long corridor to the lab. Yet I hesitated to imagine it fully. There was a fragility in the early days that made me cautious about holding on to hope.

I avoided telling most people at work, not because I was ashamed, but because I wanted to protect this tiny, forming life from the weight of the world's expectations. In the sterile glow of the lab, my secret felt like a small ember I was sheltering from the wind.

By the second trimester, I began to feel small flutters, like whispers under my skin. My energy returned in fragments. I could work longer hours without the constant pull of fatigue. My colleagues noticed a certain glow, but they could not see the undercurrent of change.

One day, as I watched a simulation of a satellite's orbital path, I realised that motherhood might be just like that: sending a part of yourself into a world you cannot fully control, hoping the systems you've built will hold. That image stayed with me. I saw the parallels everywhere: the careful preparation, the patience in development, the leap of faith when the time comes.

I also became more attuned to my body's demands. I took the elevator instead of the stairs, carried smaller loads, and drank more water. I noticed every sensation, not with fear, but with a growing awareness that my life was no longer only mine.

By the seventh month, a piece of news arrived that bent my balance beyond repair. A dear friend, also pregnant, had lost her child and then her life to the virus. The grief struck like a stone dropped into still water, rippling through my days and nights. I imagined her plans, her preparations, the way she must have counted weeks as I did, and how suddenly they had been erased.

That was the day I decided to take leave. I would close my chapter of active duty earlier than planned. The safety of my child and my own life could no longer be negotiable.

The weeks before my leave were a strange kind of farewell. There was no formal send-off, no gathering in the conference room, only small exchanges at a distance. I moved through the lab with deliberate steps, collecting files, handing over projects to colleagues, and explaining the quirks of data sets I had nurtured for months. Each handover felt like giving away a seedling I had planted myself, trusting it to another's care.

After lunch, I would wander out with my team into the majestic corridors of the campus, our pace unhurried after the intensity of the control room. The pathways meandered beneath old trees whose branches stretched wide like protective arms, casting a mesmerising play of light on the ground. We conversed in fragments, half-formed jokes and unfinished stories, words that mattered less than the awe-inspiring rhythm of walking together. Sometimes the breeze would carry the faint scent of wet earth or blossoms from the gardens, and in those moments the campus seemed alive, breathing with us. I knew I would miss this as much as the work itself: the awe-inspiring companionship, the laughter that rose and dissolved like birds taking flight, and the solace of a landscape that had become part of our shared rhythm.

Leaving felt like stepping out of orbit. I had been part of something bigger than myself, a constellation of minds working toward shared dreams. Now I was moving toward a different gravity.

From the day my pregnancy was confirmed, preparation became my quiet ritual. Between reviewing documents and attending virtual meetings, I browsed for baby essentials, tiny socks, soft bedding, and clothes folded like whispers of a life I could not yet see.

By the ninth month, my hospital bag was zipped and ready in the corner of my room. Inside were clothes for me, outfits for the baby, and small comforts for an unknown journey. The bag felt like a bridge between the life I knew and the life I was about to step into.

Motherhood began without the warmth of cultural rituals. No relatives crowded the hospital corridor, and no visitors were at home with sweets and blessings. There was the cry of a newborn breaking the sterile air, the ache of surgery in my body, and the knowledge that nothing would be the same.

The hospital smelled of sanitiser and caution. Nurses moved briskly, speaking through masks, their eyes the only visible expression. My husband was there, but our contact with others was minimal. When I held my son for the first time, swaddled and squirming, his cry was fierce and fragile all at once.

I thought of all the missions I had worked on, the precise plans and the calculated risks that had defined so much of my journey. Yet nothing I had faced before could compare with this moment. It was an experience so rare and profound that it lifted me beyond the familiar boundaries of the world I knew, leaving me awed by its sheer magnitude.

The first months were a blur of need and exhaustion. Feeding, changing, soothing, repeating. Sleep became a luxury measured in minutes. Meals were rushed or forgotten. My body healed slowly; my mind healed even slower still. I had managed critical projects under pressure, but this was different. There were no control rooms, no teams to share the load.

I often felt invisible. The focus was on the baby, as it should be, but somewhere in that shift, I became a background figure. My aches, my exhaustion, my moments of doubt were rarely acknowledged.

One dawn, after a night of almost no sleep, I sat in the dim light of the bedroom with my son in my arms. His cries had finally quieted into soft hiccups. My hair was a mess, my eyes stung with tiredness, and my back ached from holding him for hours. Yet in that silence, he opened his tiny fist and rested it on my chest as if claiming his place. In that moment, something anchored in me. This was my mission now, raw, relentless, unglamorous, but profoundly mine.

Small victories mattered. The first time he slept for more than three hours in a row felt like a miracle. The day he held his head steady without wobbling felt like a triumph. These moments were my new milestones, proof that we were both learning and growing together.

As my son grew, I grew with him. His first smile broke over me like the morning sun, and his first steps felt like a victory we celebrated together. I began to see that motherhood was not the end of who I had been, but the widening of it. The scientist, the engineer, the professional who once looked only to the stars still lived within me, steady and whole. Yet alongside her emerged the mother, the protector, the guide, ready to meet the endless needs of a small boy whose world would be shaped by the eyes that turned to me for comfort, knowledge, and love.

Returning to professional work brought delays. My promotion was postponed. My calendar no longer belonged entirely to me. Some days, work claimed me; other days, my child did. Balance, I learned, is not a static point but a shifting rhythm.

Leaving active office duty did not mean leaving behind my skills. The discipline, precision, and patience I had developed became the scaffolding for a new role. I began mentoring younger colleagues, guiding them through technical challenges and helping them navigate the unspoken rules of research life.

Mentoring Story 1:

When a young technician joined our laboratory, I could see both eagerness and hesitation in him, and his first days were marked by minor errors that could easily have been magnified into insecurity had they been met with criticism. I chose instead to treat those mistakes as stepping stones, standing beside him as he repeated each procedure until skill replaced doubt and confidence began to take root. Over time, I encouraged him not just to carry out instructions but to think about the science behind them, to ask why a method worked and what more could be discovered if he pushed further. Slowly, his questions grew bolder, his work steadier, and one day, he asked me if I thought he was capable of pursuing higher studies. I told him that the very fact he was asking showed he was ready, and in his eyes I saw the same spark that had once pushed me forward in my own journey. When he finally decided to continue his education, it felt like a triumph not only of skill but of trust, a reminder that the essence of mentorship lies in helping someone believe in themselves until they can carry that belief on their own.

Mentoring Story 2:

A fresh graduate entered our laboratory, wide-eyed and full of enthusiasm, but also a little overwhelmed by the unfamiliar atmosphere of high-end scientific research. She absorbed every instruction with care and was always eager to assist, especially during simulation work where attention to detail was essential. What struck me most was her willingness to listen, to repeat processes until she understood not just how to perform them, but why they mattered. In an environment that exposed her to cutting-edge technologies, I saw the potential for her to grow far beyond routine tasks. During our conversations, I encouraged her to envision a broader future in STEM, reminding her that every woman who chooses this path helps strengthen the bridge across the gender gap in science and engineering. Guiding her was not only about training her hands for precision, but also about nurturing her vision for what she could become and how her presence could shape the field for those who would follow.

Knowledge is not diminished by sharing. It multiplies. In mentoring, I found a continuation of my work, a legacy that would outlast my time in the lab.

Motherhood had altered my gravity. The pull of my life shifted, my balance changed forever. Yet I did not fall. I adapted, adjusted my stance, and learned to walk in a new orbit.

There is peace in acceptance. I am still the woman whose heart races as data confirms a satellite's path. I am also the woman who now stands by a crib, watching her child sleep, feeling a pride that needs no applause.

One role launches machines into the heavens. The other launches a soul into the world. Both are acts of creation. Both require vision, patience, and courage.

The scientist in me still loves the certainty of trajectories. The mother in me embraces the unpredictability of growth. Together, they make me whole.

Gravity changed. I did not fall. I found a new way to stand.

Chapter 14: The Letter I Deserved Then

"Be who you needed when you were younger."

Ayesha Siddiqi, Los Angeles based playwright of Pakistani-American descent

There is an unmatched grace in turning inward and offering yourself the silence to be heard. In a world driven by urgency and validation, self-reflection becomes a sanctuary, a soft lantern lit within the chambers of your being. It is here, in the still hush of honest reckoning, that you begin to trace the forgotten fingerprints of your journey. Writing a letter to oneself is not a ritual of regret but an offering of recognition. It is where the neglected child within is seen, the unspoken ache is named, and the quiet triumphs are finally applauded. You do not rewrite the script of your life; you illuminate it. In that sacred act, you stitch together memory and meaning, fragility and faith. Introspection is not an indulgence; it is soul maintenance. Each time you choose to listen to your innermost voice, no matter how faint, you rise in communion with your most authentic self, and that is how you begin to live fully, with gentleness, with clarity, and with courage reclaimed.

Some letters are never meant to be sent. They are written so that the heart may finally breathe, so that long-silent wounds may find the light, be acknowledged with tenderness, and begin to heal. Over the years, I have poured myself into projects and deadlines, stretched my energy to meet expectations, and found profound joy in helping my parents shape the dream of a home they longed for. I have tried, in small and steady ways, to be of use to those around me. I have also stood behind podiums and spoken to crowds, written pages filled with science and reason, nurtured a child with both strength and vulnerability, and endured the bitter bite of snow with more courage than I once believed I possessed. And yet, through all those seasons of change and becoming, something gentle but insistent remained: a modest longing to reach back through time and hold the hand of the girl I once was.

I think of her often. A teenager at Navodaya, sitting quietly beneath the spreading branches of a neem tree during evening study hour, her pencil dancing in the margins of her notebook, turning empty spaces into galaxies. Her face held the softness of someone still learning the shape of the world, yet her eyes already carried the weight of responsibility. She did not cry easily, but when unkind words found her, they carved deep and invisible wounds. She was gentle and eager to please, filled with hope and an unspoken hunger for belonging. Yet she was also far too hard on herself, too calm when she should have spoken, and far too quick to believe that love and worth had to be earned through perfection.

I often wish that someone had written her a letter. Not to correct her or offer advice, but to surround her with love: steadfast, gentle, and free from expectation. I wish she had received words that told her she was already enough, exactly as she was, even in her fears, even in her silence, even when she felt unseen.

So today, I am writing that letter. Kindness travels across years, and it is never too late to give your younger self the words she was once denied. I want her to know she was never alone, that the tenderness she longed for was always something she deserved. I want her to understand that the stars she sketched in secret were never far from her reach; they lived inside her all along.

And even now, they still do.

~

Dear Tamannah,

You do not know it yet, but the girl sitting beneath the vast sky at Navodaya, with ink on her fingers and stars sketched in the corners of her notebook, is already becoming someone extraordinary. She is becoming the woman who will carry stories, dreams, and unassuming strength through the years to come.

You are not too reticent, too soft, or lacking anything. You are exactly what you need to be. The world may not always make space for your voice, but that does not mean you should silence it. One day, your voice will help others stand with courage and speak their truth.

I remember the way you tie your plaits each morning with careful hands, trying to keep every strand in place. I remember how gently you pin your ID card above your heart as if the world will see it and understand how much effort you carry. I remember how you practice your smile in the mirror, even when your chest feels heavy with things you cannot put into words.

I see how you watch Mummy eat every night and how that muted image burns itself into your memory. I know you whisper to yourself that one day, she will rest first and that life will become easier for her. I feel your longing to make Papa proud, and I know how much you want to be seen, not just for your results but for your effort. I feel the sting when someone dismisses your hard work and the silent pride that grows inside you when your name is called during morning assembly.

You have learned to be strong and taught yourself not to ask for help. You keep your pain tucked away, hidden in the spaces where no one thinks to look. I wish someone had told you that being gentle is not something to fix; it's something to cultivate. You do not need to be loud to be powerful, and you do not need to earn your worth through exhaustion. Saying no does not make you unkind. Wanting rest does not make you weak. Feeling deeply does not make you broken. These things are part of your strength, even if others cannot see it yet.

One day, you will understand that rest is something you deserve, not something you must fight for. You will learn that boundaries are not signs of distance but signs of self-respect. You will carry your softness like silk, not as something fragile, but as something graceful and full of life. You will walk with delicate confidence; your steps infused with wisdom and a beauty that does not demand attention.

There will be days when you stumble. There will be nights when your tears fall freely on the bathroom floor, and no one will know. You will lose people you once held close, and your heart will ache from the emptiness that follows. You will doubt yourself while questioning your place in the world. But you will also stand in bright rooms where your voice is heard. You will hold your child in your arms and feel a love so vast it softens every wound. You will make choices that protect your peace, even if others do not understand them. You will become the woman you once dreamed of meeting.

You will learn to forgive the people who did not understand you. More importantly, you will learn to forgive yourself. You will forgive yourself for trusting too quickly, for staying silent when you need to speak, and for forgetting that you, too, are allowed to rest, to feel, and to grow.

You will become more than what you ever imagined. You will build a home where love feels steady, not loud. You will teach your kids that kindness does not mean invisibility and that thier voice has value even when it shakes. When you see a young girl with quiet eyes and the same questions you once carried, you will pause. You will look at her with warmth, and you will say the words you always needed to hear.

You will tell her that she is enough. That her gentleness is not a weakness. That she does not have to exhaust herself to be loved. That she can protect her peace. That her voice matters, even in its softest form.

This letter is neither a goodbye nor an apology. It is a love letter across time and, more specifically, the hand of the woman you have become, reaching back to hold the girl who was always trying her best.

You were never alone. Not then. Not now.

With pride, with grace, and with all the healing we have gathered together,

Your future self

~

Writing this letter did not just bring peace. It gave voice to a tranquil part of me that had waited for years to be seen, to be held, and to be honoured. That younger version of myself, so full of questions and courage, walked through uncertainty with unmatched grace. She did not have applause, but she had a purpose. She did not ask for recognition, but she gave everything she had.

In her hushed strength, in her private battles, in her small triumphs that no one noticed, she built the woman I am today. Her silence became my resilience. Her longing became my direction. Her patience shaped my values.

If ever she looks back and wonders whether the waiting, the hoping, and the effort were worth it, I want her to know this truth clearly and tenderly. Yes, it was. Every part of it was necessary. She did not just survive. She became the reason I can now stand tall.

She is not just a memory but a foundation. She is the fire. In every step I take forward, I carry her with pride, with gratitude, and with the understated promise that she will never be forgotten again.

Chapter 15: What I Would Tell Her Today

We are often led to believe that a life's worth is measured in titles, salaries, and the applause it garners. However, the truth is far more profound. It's the small, unseen moments that truly endure. The decisions made when no one is watching, the kindness given without an audience, the courage chosen when it would have been easier to turn away. These are the moments that shape a life and leave a lasting impact. A nation is not built by grand speeches or towering monuments alone. It is built in kitchens where someone feeds a hungry neighbour before themselves, in classrooms where a teacher stays late to help a child who is falling behind, in the way we choose to treat each other when nothing is at stake except our humanity. Living morally is not just a choice; it's a service to humanity. If you can live so that your absence is felt in the everyday goodness of others, then you have already served in the highest way possible.

On a summer evening in Odisha, long before my name ever appeared on an office door, I was sitting at a small railway station waiting for a train that had been delayed for over an hour. The platform was warm under my feet. The air was heavy with the smell of chai simmering in dented aluminium kettles, and from somewhere nearby came the faint clang of a blacksmith's hammer. On the bench beside me sat a woman with a child in her lap. She had one cloth bag and a steel tiffin box, and her sari pallu was wrapped around the boy's waist as if to keep him from slipping. He was restless, pulling at her bangles, kicking his bare feet against the bench. She opened the tiffin to quiet him, and inside were only a few rotis and a little paper cone of salt. She tore off a piece, dipped it in the salt and handed it to him, her hunger folded away behind a smile that didn't quite reach her eyes.

Without thinking too much about it, I reached into my bag and took out the small packet of biscuits I had bought earlier. I walked over and offered it to her. She looked at me for a moment, then took it and gave it to the boy without a word. He tore the packet open and began eating with the single-minded focus only children have. She murmured a blessing I could barely hear, still not looking directly at me. I went back to my bench and sat down. It was a small thing, biscuits worth hardly anything, but I remember feeling lighter as I watched them. I had not done anything heroic, yet I had made a moment softer for someone else. That was the first time I understood that service is not measured by scale but by the weight it carries in the instant it is given.

Over the years, I have seen that the most enduring acts of service are often the quietest. There were projects in my career where my name never appeared in the final credits. My part was hidden in the middle of the work, in calibrating an instrument so another scientist could get accurate readings, in checking one more set of numbers at midnight because something seemed slightly off, and in reviewing a colleague's report so they could present it without error. These were not the moments anyone photographed or celebrated. They were the moments that made the larger picture stronger. They taught me to be content with the knowledge that the mission was better because of my unseen hand.

When I became a mother, I learned that service could be both invisible and endless. There were nights when my body ached from holding my son for hours, telling the same story over and over because it was the only way he would sleep. I also ate cold leftovers so he could have the hot meal. No one clapped for these things. There was no audience and no headlines. But they shaped him, and they shaped me. Service is not only about giving what you have. Sometimes it is about sharing what you are.

If I could speak to the girl I was in those early hostel years, the one who sat on the steps with a half-empty purse and more questions than answers, I would tell her that her worth would never be in the things she collected. It would be in the things she planted. Plant trust in people. Plant dignity in your work. Plant courage in yourself. Some seeds will sprout quickly. Some will take years. Some you will never see bloom. Plant them anyway.

I have met young women who believe they must wait until they are essential before they can serve. They think they need the right job, the right badge, the right applause. I tell them the same thing I wish someone had told me. Do not wait. Service does not begin when the stage is ready. It starts in the moment you decide to step forward. You can serve with your mind, with your hands, with your words, with your presence. You can begin now, with whatever you have, wherever you are.

There is a strange kind of courage in showing up for the world when it has not asked you to. Sometimes you will be welcomed, ignored, sometimes even ridiculed. Walk forward anyway. The road will never be obvious. There will be loose stones under your feet, and some days it will feel like the climb is too steep. Keep walking. Your balance will grow with every step, and your strength will come from the act of moving despite your fear.

Serving the nation is not limited to government buildings or official duty. The country is divided into smaller places, too. It lives in the breath of elders giving their blessings in a village courtyard. It lives in the smell of wet earth after the first monsoon rain. It lives in the patience of a schoolteacher in a dusty classroom. It lives in the honesty of a farmer weighing his grain under the shade of a tree. Every quiet act of integrity is an act of nation-building, even if no one notices it.

I have seen India from many corners; from the narrow lanes of my village to the clean corridors of space research centres, from the bustling markets of Ahmedabad to the frozen vastness of Antarctica. No matter where I stood, I carried the same instinct: to show up. Show up for the person who needs your knowledge. Show up for the neighbour who needs your time. Show up for yourself, so that you do not forget that your well-being matters too. This is how service continues, not in the shadow of your career, but in the centre of your everyday choices.

Legacy is not the weight of a medal or the length of a résumé. It is the path you leave clear enough for someone else to walk. When I look back, I do not see only the projects or the titles. I see faces: the boy in Ladakh who asked his first question about the stars, my sister who stepped into her dream because I kept the light on for her, and the colleague who found her confidence because I stood still while she learned to stand. These moments are my legacy and footprints I hope will guide someone else forward.

If I were to stand before the girl I once was, the young woman chasing marks, the scientist running between deadlines, I would tell her that everything she gives will matter, though not always in the way she expects. The day she stops chasing credit will be the day she serves without fear. And when the applause fades, when the desk is cleared, when her name is no longer called in meetings, what will remain will be the way she made people feel, the courage she stirred in them, the doors she held open. That will be her real work.

I do not know where you will be when you read these words. You might be on a bus to a city where you see no one. You might be at a desk in a quiet office. You might be standing by a pond in your village. Wherever you are, I hope you remember that service is not a chapter that ends. It is a way of breathing. You carry it in how you live, in how you treat others, in how you hold yourself steady in the storms.

There was a morning in Antarctica when I stood alone outside the research station. The light was so clear it felt like you could see to the end of the world. The wind pressed against my face. Around me, there was nothing but snow and sky, no sound except my breath. I thought of the railway station in Odisha, the woman with her child, the biscuits in my hand; two moments, worlds apart, yet carrying the same truth. Service is not about where you are. It is about who you choose to be. And it is always your choice.

One day, my voice will fade from the rooms where I once spoke, and my hands will no longer hold the work they carried for so many years. But somewhere a young woman will take a step she was afraid to take, a child will look at the night sky with new wonder, or a neighbour will choose kindness over indifference, and I will be there in a way no one can see. That is the quiet promise of a life lived in service; it does not end when we do. It moves forward, carried in the hearts of those we once touched, finding new hands, new voices, and new mornings to begin again.

That is what I would tell her today. And that is what I will say to you now.

Verses Kindler Publication

Reach us through our website -

https://www.verseskindlerpublication.com/

For more information visit our

Instagram or Facebook page.

9 789347 494253

Printed at Repro India Ltd.